Blades, Blood and Bandages

Nov 2012

Blades, Blood and Bandages

The Experiences of People who Self-injure

Theresa McShane
Queen's University, Belfast

palgrave
macmillan

First published 2012 by
PALGRAVE MACMILLAN

Palgrave Macmillan in the UK is an imprint of Macmillan Publishers Limited, registered in England, company number 785998, of Houndmills, Basingstoke, Hampshire RG21 6XS.

Palgrave Macmillan in the US is a division of St Martin's Press LLC, 175 Fifth Avenue, New York, NY 10010.

Palgrave Macmillan is the global academic imprint of the above companies and has companies and representatives throughout the world.

Palgrave® and Macmillan® are registered trademarks in the United States, the United Kingdom, Europe and other countries

ISBN: 978–0–230–25281–3

This book is printed on paper suitable for recycling and made from fully managed and sustained forest sources. Logging, pulping and manufacturing processes are expected to conform to the environmental regulations of the country of origin.

A catalogue record for this book is available from the British Library.

A catalog record for this book is available from the Library of Congress.

10 9 8 7 6 5 4 3 2 1
21 20 19 18 17 16 15 14 13 12

Printed and bound in the United States of America

To John

Contents

Tables

Acknowledgements

Throughout the time spent talking to people who self-injure and writing this book, I was helped by many people whom I would like to acknowledge and thank. First and foremost to the participants of this study, thank you for taking part and for helping me to understand self-injury. I know that for many of you the emotional effort required to share your stories with me was enormous and I will forever be indebted. Thank you also to the participants who gave permission for selections of poetry to be used in the book. Thank you Tracie Cupples for your interest and involvement. To Dr Pauline Prior (Senior Lecturer in Social Policy at Queen's University, Belfast), thank you so much for all the time, help and encouragement you have given me; for the many 'marathon meetings' in your office and your living room; and for your understanding and patience, especially when things were not going so well. Thanks to Professors Robert Miller (Professor of Sociology, Queen's University, Belfast) and Gerhard Riemann (Professor of Social Work, University of Bamberg, Germany) for some much appreciated comments in the early stages of the work. To Jim Walsh, thank you for your assistance in contacting participants and facilitating interviews. A word of thanks to my special friends – Anne Furgrove, Kathy Donnelly and Lorraine Boyd – for our lunchtime 'complaining/therapy sessions'. Thanks to Kathleen McShane, whose comments were invaluable during some difficult days. To Maureen McShane for all your help with baby Michael, I can't thank you enough. Do mo léitheoir profaí Séamus MacAindreasa: A chara dhílis, gabhaim gach buíochas as ucht do chuid tacaíocht agus cuidiú uilig. Go raibh go céad maith agat. Thanks to my brothers and sisters for the regular enquiries of 'How's it goin?' To my mother Marie Curran, thank you for all the babysitting, the dinner making, the general encouragement and the multi-vitamins. To my children, Darren, Paul, Katie and Michael McShane – thanks kids for all your help around the house, for putting up with no living room for months and for generally driving me mad/cheering me on. Finally, to my husband John McShane... Thank you for being my computer technician... For looking after the kids, me, the house... For

ix

supporting and encouraging me ... For listening to me and pretending to be interested ... Words can't do justice to all you have done for me ... Thank you!

Study participants gave permission for extracts from their poetry, diaries and interview transcripts to be used in this publication. If any copyright holder has been inadvertently overlooked, the publishers will be pleased to make the necessary arrangements at the earliest opportunity.

A Note on Language

People who self-injure are diverse. Although they may share with one another a number of life commonalities, they also vary in individual characteristics and distinctiveness. Throughout this book I have avoided use of the term 'self-injurer' or any other reference that names or categorises a group of people according to a description of behaviour. Instead, I refer to the people who took part using language such as 'people who self-injure' or 'self-injuring individuals'. Exceptional use of terms such as 'self-injurer', 'self-harmer' and 'cutter' are used only in reference to direct speech, usually by participants themselves, where such use is deemed necessary to illustrate meanings and experiences of self-injury, particularly regarding stigma.

1
Introduction

'Blades, blood and bandages' [by Sally]

Seeing is believing
Isn't that what they say?
Who are they that say that?
What is it that they mean?

For me, it's true in a way
For when I see I understand
I take my blade and I incise
In a vain attempt to exorcise

The cut not reason for the pain
The blood, the symbol of deep shame
Bandages, gentle balm that soothes
Right then I understand

Perhaps, if you could see
Then you would believe
Or maybe understand, not judge me,
My blades, my blood and my bandages

Can you imagine feeling so emotionally distressed that you lift a blade and draw it across the skin on your arm? You do not want to die. You want to feel better. The action may be spontaneous and chaotic. More likely it is controlled and precise. The first bead of blood appears under the blade and with it a huge surge of relief from unbearable internal turmoil. You may feel guilt afterwards because you know it is not acceptable behaviour, but you cannot help yourself. It may even be that this small blade will prevent you from reaching the point of suicide. This is self-injury and the topic of this book. Not only this. It is self-injury from the perspective of people who self-injure. It is their experiences, their meanings, their accounts using their words.

Protection of oneself from pain and injury is considered a central tenet of human existence. Why then do some of us cut our own skin with blades or burn ourselves with cigarette lighters? What would bring a person to bang himself off a wall or refuse to let her own wounds heal? The act of self-injury forces us to question some of our most deeply held beliefs about life and the preservation of health and well-being. Self-injury, as depicted by the people who spoke to me, is the non-suicidal infliction of injury and/or pain on the self. Often people who self-injure will do so by cutting their arms, sometimes their hands, legs and abdomen, as well as other less commonly used parts of the body, such as the face and genitals. Besides cutting, people may burn, hit, scald, pinch, or bang themselves off hard surfaces.

There are numerous books available on the topic of self-injury, most of which are written from medical backgrounds, many illustrated with examples of self-injuring clients. As a result, the dominant presentation of self-injury is one rooted in psychopathology. The perspective of the individual who self-injures is under-represented. So too is our understanding of self-injuring people who do not come into contact with medical services and professionals. *Blades, Blood and Bandages: The Experiences of People who Self-injure* is an attempt to redress the balance somewhat, by offering an alternative to the medical perspective. Twenty-five people, who have self-injured, shared with me their experiences and this book is centred around their testimonies. Although they were not drawn from a clinical population, some had crossed paths with medical authorities in relation to their self-injury. People who self-injure can offer comprehensive and discerning insights into the behaviour. Although each person who spoke to me had a unique story and set of experiences to share, when given an opportunity to talk freely about their self-injury and issues important to them, common themes emerged. Discussions centred around the three broad topics of suffering, stigma and ritual. Because the position of the individual has been neglected, these themes have been under investigated in the study of self-injury. In presenting their experiences, I have drawn upon other published work on self-injury and have conceptualised the discussions in chapters 4, 5 and 6 with sociological theories pertaining to suffering, stigma and ritual.

The first part of the book introduces self-injury by discussing the main approaches to the topic including what is already acknowledged about the behaviour and those who practise it. The people who took part in this book are introduced in Chapter 3. They were recruited from the general public, using newspaper and poster advertisements posing the simple question 'Please help me understand self-injury'. Some of the reasons given for taking part were: 'I wanted to help people understand about self-injury'; 'I know how lonely it is when you think you are the only person in the world who does this and I want to tell other people who self-injure that they are not alone'. Each person took part in a one-to-one interview with me. As well as rich interview material from all participants, three also wrote diaries of self-injury and a further three contributed selections of poetry written during times of deep emotional turmoil. These creative expressions of the experience of self-injury are interspersed throughout the discussion and each chapter opens with a poetry extract.

Childhood trauma and sexual abuse are often considered factors associated with subsequent self-injury in medical studies. This was also the case in this study as over half of the participants revealed themselves to have been sexually abused in childhood. Others suffered severe physical and emotional trauma. However, another less obvious form of disrupted bonding in childhood was that of emotional invalidation, whereby the expression of emotions is denied or punished. The role of suffering in the life of someone who self-injures is the topic of Chapter 4 and is conceptualised using the sociological theory of 'trajectory' (Riemann and Schütze, 2005). Using this framework, we can see how self-injury often begins and is maintained as a way to escape from, and exert a degree of control over, the emotional impact of one's life circumstances that seem to be driven by uncontrollable outer forces (at least in the beginning). Steve is a 40-year-old ex-soldier who had been sexually, physically and emotionally abused in childhood. In common with many who took part in the study, he was severely affected by negative experiences in childhood from adults in caregiving roles. He describes how he 'grew up always being treated as a total waste of space'.

The intensity and depth of the interviews allowed much rich information to emerge, so much so, a little known aspect of self-injury, the ritual, was brought to light. Self-injury can become a highly ritualised behaviour, yet this aspect has received very little research attention. Chapter 5 presents the relationship between self-injury and ritual, an association involving a process of complex, multilayered interaction involving practical and symbolic levels. Steve describes his self-injury ritual:

> There was a real structure to it. It's always in the evening. It's always with a razor blade and the notion would come on me about two or three days before it. And then I would prepare my self-harm equipment. I would start thinking about it and then I would try to distract myself. But the thoughts actually become really intense because I'm really emotional you know…It's hard to describe…Really agitated. And then I would start preparing for it. I'd have loads of kitchen roll [absorbent material], new blades every time…I'd be really clinical and clean about it. Sometimes I'd buy bandages…um…antiseptic liquid…and I'd be just sitting there in the living room with everything prepared…And I'd start thinking. [Steve]

Self-injury rituals can appear to be simple routines involving nothing more than the need to use a specific implement, such as a blade, or preference for a particular time of day in which to self-injure. Equally, rituals may be complex and like Steve's, can take days to complete and include a range of equipment and elaborate preparation. Therapeutic counsellors may find this section particularly interesting as the ritualistic role of self-injury is significant in the establishment and continuation of the behaviour. Rituals have already been identified in the social sciences. In relation to drug use, for example, the focus is on the complex relationship between the individual and the needle as part of the drug using experience (McBride et al., 2001). *Blades, Blood and Bandages* makes comparable observations in its exploration of how people who self-injure become fixated on many aspects in the self-injury ritual. This infatuation can manifest itself in three main guises. First, relationships with apparatus, such as blades, cleaning equipment and music can become part of the practice. Second, surroundings, including bedrooms or other private spaces may be necessities in the ritual. Third, procedures may be followed along a particular routine, involving gathering equipment, ensuring privacy and allowing intense emotions to build. All these elements may be enveloped into a sophisticated ceremony of self-injury. The ritual may be short, or it can span days either side of the actual episode of physical injury. Physical senses are involved in the ritual. One's sight, hearing, touch, taste and smell can all be stimulated. Psychological and physical functions are combined. It would seem, therefore, that self-injury is an extreme but effective 'work-out' for the emotion and sensory systems.

Self-injury is costly to the person who practises it in a number of ways and these costs are the focus of Chapter 6. It is a highly stigmatised behaviour as Dawn, a 21-year-old student illustrates: 'I felt better after [self-injuring] and then about ten minutes later I started to feel bad about it, cos I thought "God, I have to wear long sleeves now for the next week"'. Stigma was experienced by everyone who took part in the book, to varying degrees. People who self-injure are caught between the temporary relief self-injury brings and a strong awareness of society's rejection of the behaviour. Self-injury is a highly stigmatised behaviour, a fact which adds considerably to the suffering of those who practise it. Yet this aspect of the behaviour is almost totally ignored in its study. *Blades, Blood and Bandages* looks in detail at the stigma of self-injury as reported by people who have experienced it. Speaking to those who self-injure reveals that they are not only stigmatised by the negative treatment received from non-self-injuring people (including those in the medical profession), but also, more complexly, by their own *fear* of such treatment. Indeed it is this dread of negative reaction from others which can promote a complex series of stigma management techniques aimed at avoiding and minimising stigma. The book draws on other works on stigma including those of classic theorists such as Goffman (1963) and on the work of stigmatised behaviour in other social realms. Comparisons with Scambler and Hopkins' (1986) examination of stigma and epilepsy, for example, are useful in the attempt to understand stigma in the sphere of self-injury. The lives of people who self-injure can be adversely affected in many areas. Chapter 6, in addition to tackling stigma, addresses other social costs incurred by people who self-injure. Relationship problems, social paralysis and vulnerability to other forms of self-harm are examined.

It is possible to move away from self-injury and Chapter 7 examines how people who are successful in this process manage to do so. People cannot be forced into stopping. Rather, if certain conditions are implemented, the need for self-injury can reduce of its own accord. Therapeutic disclosure to sympathetic others can open up opportunities to reflect on one's situation. Sally, a 32-year-old differently abled woman, abused as a child by a family member, gives an example:

> They [rape counsellors] just accept that that's your way of coping...They listen to what it does for you...They help you work through why you cut...what it means to you and the whole process...Then you grow to understand it yourself. [Sally]

It can then be possible to make changes in how one views one's state of affairs. The concept of 'accounting' (Goffman, 1963) is useful in helping us understand how people attempt to make their situation more bearable. Techniques of accounting to others and to oneself at this stage are employed for purposes of redefinition in two main areas. First, they are used by the individual to redefine self-injury in order to de-stigmatise it. Some of the ways in which people try to redefine their self-injury is to compare it to other, more socially acceptable, forms of self-harm, such as alcohol abuse or obesity. Sally assessed this similarity as 'Eaters eat, drinkers drink and cutters cut'. Another strategy is to criticise as hypocritical those in society who would stigmatise them. Some people may also become politically active. Striving to improve the public image of people who self-injure, in addition to benefiting others, can decrease the stigma felt by the political activist and simultaneously raise their self-worth. The second area for redefinition is to change one's perspective of one's suffering in order to, where possible, make painful memories less intense. Ella, for example, in accounting reasons for her mother's failure to stop her father sexually abusing her, was able to forgive her and, in doing so, lessen her own suffering.

Everyone who took part in the book reported experiences of overwhelming negative emotions. Moreover, they had all employed harmful emotion regulation techniques. The first of these was often suppression, whereby they tried to control unwanted emotions and feelings by forcing themselves to 'not feel' and 'not think' them, or attempting to simply push them away. Other harmful emotion regulation techniques to follow suppression were self-injury and for some, alcohol and/or drug use in addition. About a third of those interviewed were no longer self-injuring when we spoke. Among this group, it was commonly stated that the best way of getting rid of negative emotions was first to accept them for what they were. Doing this took time and practice and was often punctuated with relapses into self-injury along the way. Some of those who managed to move away from self-injury reported that natural processes of maturation contributed to their ability to take more control over their lives and they were also less likely to be restricted by role expectations which constrained them while younger. As a result, the need to self-injure was diminished. Positive techniques of distraction were numerous and included avoidance of reminders of suffering, exercise and responsibilities to dependants.

The final chapter of the book takes a wider, societal view of self-injury and identifies its changing social face. Over the past decade, self-injury has emerged from obscurity to its current position as a topic which is more highly visible. The social face of self-injury is changing due to the influence of the media and the internet. People who begin to self-injure today are now more likely to have heard or read about it prior to trying it themselves. They are less isolated now than in previous decades and although the behaviour is still highly stigmatised, it is becoming less so. Chapter 8 examines self-injury in popular culture and the role of the multimedia.

This book is not written by a medical scholar, although medical scholars may find it a refreshing alternative to books written from within the medical perspective. It is not meant as a self-help book, although reading about the experiences of people who self-injure may offer hope to others in similar positions and greater understanding in general to anyone who wants to know about the meaning of self-injury. I believe that investigating self-injury from the perspective of the individual in a non-medical setting is fundamental to developing a deep understanding of the behaviour. Self-injury is a complex and multilayered phenomenon and people who use it are more diverse than in the picture so far presented. I consider myself extremely privileged to have been entrusted with the deeply personal and intimate stories of the people who took part in my research. This book is a representation of self-injury from their perspective. It is testament to the belief that the best way to understand self-injury is to ask people who self-injure. I hope to have represented them accurately.

The main findings discussed in chapters 4 to 8 are summarised as follows:

The role of suffering (Chapter 4)

- Self-injury often begins and is maintained in response to suffering.
- Self-injury from the perspective of those who practise it can be viewed as a non-suicidal response to psychological distress. The purpose of self-injury can be to temporarily escape from, or to take control of, what can be referred to as a trajectory of suffering. The trajectory of suffering may originate from trauma experienced in childhood (e.g. sexual and/or physical abuse), but more commonly as a response to a less obvious form of disrupted bonding – that of invalidation.

Self-injury rituals (Chapter 5)

- Self-injury can become a highly ritualised behaviour involving equipment, surroundings and procedures.
- It is an extreme but therapeutic workout for the emotion and sensory systems.

Stigma and damaged lives (Chapter 6)

- Self-injury is a highly stigmatised behaviour, not only in relation to negative treatment from others (enacted stigma), but also in terms of the more complex fear of negative treatment (felt stigma) This book presents an in-depth account of the experience of stigma including how people employ techniques of stigma management.
- Aside from stigma, the lives of those who self-injure can be additionally adversely affected in other areas, including in terms of

their relationships with others, social paralysis and vulnerability to other forms of self-harm.

Disclosure, redefinition and resilience (Chapter 7)

- Disclosure of self-injury to sympathetic others can play an important role in opening chances to self-reflect.
- Techniques of redefinition of self-injury are employed to de-stigmatise the behaviour.
- Techniques used to redefine one's situation can lessen suffering.
- Acceptance of negative emotions can assist the move away from self-injury.
- Processes of maturation aid one's distancing oneself from self-injury.
- Strategies of distraction can support the cessation process.

Self-injury and popular culture (Chapter 8)

- Although many who self-injure begin to do so in psychological isolation from others (several report an early belief that they 'invented' it), people who begin to self-injure today are more likely than in previous decades to be introduced to it from outside sources.
- The internet and multimedia are important factors in how self-injury is learned, maintained and viewed in wider society. People who self-injure are generally less isolated nowadays than in the past. It is still a highly stigmatised behaviour but is becoming less so.

2
What Is Self-injury?

'Self-injury' [by Jane]

As I kept on tearing
The pain deadened more
And then the blood came
And I felt so overcome for a few moments
I was excited, pleased
Ashamed that I'd done this
Tears came to my eyes
But I didn't cry
I still haven't cried
So I did it again
Only a little different
Quick and Sharp
And the blood came
Not as good as the first go
But there's still time

Self-injury in a brief historical context

Many people find the topic of self-injury too disturbing to even
consider, yet for centuries references to (usually gruesome forms of)
self-injury can be found in historical, biblical and medical sources.
Favazza (1998) gives two examples:

In Book Six of the *History*, Herodotus (5th century BC) describes
the actions of a deranged, probably psychotic, Spartan leader: 'As

soon as the knife was in his hands, Cleomenes began to mutilate himself, beginning on his shins. He sliced his flesh into strips, working upwards to his thighs, hips and sides until he reached his belly, which he chopped into mincemeat'. The Gospel of Mark 5:5 describes a repetitive self-mutilator, a man who 'night and day would cry aloud among the tombs and on the hillsides and cut himself with stones'. (259)

Self-injury even then was associated with insanity, which could be linked to evil spirits (Adler and Adler, 2007; Bissland and Munger, 1985). Bloodletting as a medical or therapeutic remedy for maladies such as melancholia (depression) goes back further, extending from ancient times right up to the mid-nineteenth century (Jackson, 2008). Bloodletting was stopped when pioneering French psychiatrist Pinel put an end to the practice, ending over 2000 years of its use as a standard medical procedure (Jackson, 2008). It was not until the 1960s that it again came to medical attention in psychiatry where it has been 'trivialised (wrist-cutting), misidentified (suicide attempt), and regarded solely as a symptom (a criterion of borderline personality disorder)' (Favazza, 1998:259). Reviewing what has been written about self-injury makes it clear that much of what was known about it then and now comes from clinical studies and observations of people being treated for psychopathology (Adler and Adler, 2007, 2011).

From the 1990s, alternative opinions on self-injury began to be heard. Qualitative research (mostly carried out by psychologists) with people who self-injure began to uncover meanings and functions of the behaviour which contradicted the conventional medical model, most importantly that self-injury could be seen as a non-suicidal response to psychological distress (e.g. Favazza, 1989, 1998; Miller, 1994). Underlying psychopathology remained the dominant viewpoint in medical circles. However, the theme of childhood trauma as a factor in self-injury seemed to be common ground on which both medical opinion and personal accounts of individuals' experiences converged (e.g. Solomon and Farrand, 1996; Van der Kolk et al., 1991).

Recent sociological attention has begun to chart changes in the social meanings of self-injury due to the influence of societal factors (Adler and Adler, 2007, 2011; Hodgson, 2004). Around the same time as the accounts of individuals who self-injured were being noticed, media interest and public awareness were heightened when some celebrities, such as Princess Diana and actor Johnny Depp, admitted self-injuring. Simultaneously, there was a surge of interest in the topic from a variety of medical and non-medical quarters, including 'adolescents, young adults, educators, doctors, psychologists, and social workers' (Adler and Adler, 2007:538). This interest has grown since the appearance of internet chat rooms in the early 2000s, allowing people to 'interact anonymously but with great intimacy' (Adler and Adler, 2007:538). Self-injury, which was previously believed to arise spontaneously as a result of psychopathology, is now being considered a behaviour that is being learned from sources other than the self, under the influence of changing social structures (Adler and Adler, 2012, 2007; Hodgson, 2004). Similarly, although self-injury is still highly stigmatised, there has been a reduction in the amount of 'rejection, isolation and alienation' being experienced by people who self-injure (Adler and Adler, 2007).

In order to build on what is known about self-injury it is clear that the perspective of the individual is needed. This brings us to the main thrust of this book which states simply that the best way to understand self-injury is to ask people who self-injure. The experiences and meanings represented here are based on what 25 people who self-injure have told me in one-to-one conversations and through the written and creative word in diaries and poems.

Before we begin on this quest let us continue with a factual introduction to self-injury in order to understand how the behaviour has been presented so far. At the forefront is the issue of definitions. There is a lack of common consensus regarding what to call the behaviour, and what actions and intentions to include or exclude (especially regarding UK research), which renders problematic any attempt to draw up a comprehensive picture of the research. I have counted at least 13 different terms used to describe various actions and intentions and the list is not definitive. Defining self-injury is also affected by those aspects which separate self-injurious acts from other forms of self-harm such as the influence of cultural sanctioning, intentions of the individual and the link with suicide. All these issues will be considered followed by what is known about self-injury at both general population levels and within certain groups in society (e.g. gender and age). However, problems regarding definitions, lack of large-scale epidemiological studies on this behaviour alone and the fact that there remains a hidden population of people who self-injure have a roll-on effect when it comes to making accurate estimations.

The perspective taken in research influences the questions asked, which in turn informs what we know about the phenomenon. The question 'Why do people self-injure?' is addressed, first from the perspective of the medical model of health and illness, and then from the viewpoint of people who have direct experience of self-injuring. What is the relationship between self-injury and society? What is the effect of this relationship on how people learn and maintain self-injury? How are they affected by stigma? These are examples of questions more likely to be posed by recent sociological interest in the behaviour. Finally in this chapter a summary of theoretical stances on self-injury reveals gaps in the research. It is clear that aspects of self-injury remain unaddressed in its study. The conceptualisation of themes being considered in this book will be introduced.

Language and definitions

It may safely be assumed that people do things that are not good for them at some time or another. We may know someone, or indeed ourselves be someone, who smokes, drinks too much alcohol, over or under eats, over or under exercises, or simply neglects their emotional and physical welfare in general. We could include eating disorders, drug abuse, staying in abusive relationships, or taking seemingly senseless risks. So what makes self-injury different from other forms of self-harm? The first step in defining self-injury is the particularly daunting task of unravelling the mishmash of terms, actions intentions, inclusions and exclusions on which there is lack of universal agreement.

Self-injury is described under a variety of terms. These include: 'deliberate self-injury' (Klonsky, 2007), 'nonsuicidal self-injury', also referred to as NSSI (Klonsky and Muehlenkamp, 2007; Nixon and Health, 2009), 'self-inflicted violence' (Brown and Bryan, 2007), 'self-harm' (Abrams and Gordon, 2003; NICE, 2004), 'deliberate self-harm' (Gratz, 2001, 2006, 2007), 'deliberate self-harm syndrome' (Pattison and Kahan, 1983), 'self-mutilation' (Nock and Prinstein, 2004; Ross and Heath, 2002; Strong, 1998), 'moderate self-mutilation' (Favazza, 1989, 1996, 1998; Favazza and Rosenthal, 1993), 'parasuicide' (Ogundipe, 1999), 'self-destructive behaviour' (Van der Kolk et al., 1991), 'self-injurious behaviour' (Bowen and John, 2001; Herpertz, 1995; Shearer, 1994; Trepal, 2010; Whitlock et al., 2006a), 'self-wounding' (Sharkey, 2003; Tantam and Whittaker, 1992), 'self-cutting' (Suyemoto and MacDonald, 1995).

I have chosen to use the term self-injury as it seemed the most appropriate appellation for the phenomenon under investigation. It is the most accurate overall word that describes the behaviour and intentions presented by the people who took part in this book. It is also less likely to be conceived as judgmental (Adler and Adler, 2005; NICE, 2004) in comparison to such terms which include 'deliberate' as a prefix. The term 'self-mutilation' (a common term especially in American literature in the 1990s and early 2000s) is now considered by many authors, both those representing the viewpoint of people who self-injure and of medical professionals, to be excessive and overly suggestive (e.g. Connors, 2000; Hyman, 1999). Although wounds can vary in severity from minor scratches to those which leave permanent scars, self-injury is often not extreme enough to be described accurately as 'mutilation' and the fact that it is a coping mechanism to deal with psychological distress, according to Walsh (2008), means that there is a certain amount of adaptivity associated with the behaviour. This in no way underestimates levels of emotional disturbance and refers only to physical damage to the body. Furthermore, 'self-injury', akin to Adler and Adler's (2007) respondents, was the term most frequently used by the people who spoke to me to describe the act. This term is now the preferred term for many authors (Adler and Adler, 2005, 2007, 2011; Connors, 2000; Hyman, 1999; Hodgson, 2004; Nafisi and Stanley, 2007; Nixon and Heath, 2009; Solomon and Farrand, 1996).

With regard to particular self-injurious acts, self-injury can include most frequently, 'cutting, scratching, carving, self-hitting, self-burning, excoriation of wounds, picking, and abrading' (Walsh, 2007:1058). Some authors, in addition, will include branding and bone breaking (Adler and Adler, 2005, 2007; Favazza, 1998), biting (Adler and Adler, 2005), trichotillomania, nail biting, needle sticking and interference with wound healing (Favazza, 1998). Most people, who have reported injuring themselves, usually have more than one method (Favazza and Conterio, 1989; Gratz, 2001; Herpertz, 1995). Out of all these acts, cutting and burning would appear to be the most commonly used (Favazza, 1998). The most common site of self-injury on the body is the arm, but other places such as hands, legs, and less commonly, the face, abdomen, breasts and genitals (Babiker and Arnold, 1997). Generally excluded are extreme forms of injurious acts which Favazza refers to as 'major self-mutilation'. These include 'eye enucleation, castration, and limb amputation' (Favazza, 1998:263). Examples of other excluded actions are 'drilling holes into [one's] skull, intentionally making [oneself] ill [and] decorating [one's] body in extremely radically ways' (Adler and Adler, 2005:346).

Self-injury and culture

An important difference in how self-injury stands out from other forms of self-harm is how it is viewed in society. The behaviour is neither culturally sanctioned, nor is it culturally acceptable (Favazza, 1998). It is not promoted, as in the context of a socially approved ritual involving mutilation, as in a circumcision or other spiritual or religious rite of passage. Neither is it accepted as an unfortunate reality of life to be tolerated (if reluctantly), as in mild alcohol excesses. Although self-injury is often associated with teenage angst and anguish and within this age group there may be limited acceptance and support of the behaviour, 'there are no organised, culturally endorsed rituals that surround it. Self-injury is not connected to any socially sanctioned rite of passage' (Walsh, 2008:4).

Self-injury, control and predictability

Acts which are classified as self-injury are also characterised by the instantaneousness of results and the control and preciseness with which they can be delivered. For example, self-poisoning is excluded from many definitions of self-injury (usually in studies based on meanings of self-injury from the perspective of those who practise it) as this method of self-harm can be difficult to control and the effects are expected to arise more gradually. Forms of self-injury however, especially cutting, are characterised by their predictability, their instantaneousness, and they are usually more likely to be controllable in their implementation. They 'may be more immediately and more dramatically destructive than these other forms of self-harm (though not necessarily more dangerous long-term)' (Bristol Crisis Service for Women, 2000:3).

Self-injury and suicide

The term 'deliberate self-harm' is a commonly used term, especially in British medical studies, to describe a broad range of self-harming behaviours which include for example, self-injury *and* self-poisoning (Hawton et al., 2002). Often these studies do not specify intent of participants regarding suicide. Attempts to review some medical literature in relation to self-injury only is extremely problematic as the 'umbrella' term 'deliberate self-harm' subsumes self-injury as a sub-category. Self-poisoning and self-injury may have different meanings for those who have used these behaviours (Solomon and Farrand, 1996; Walsh, 2008). For example, an act of 'deliberate self-harm' can range from a serious attempt to die, such as jumping from a height, to a superficial cut made to the arm in which no suicidal ideation is intended. In addition, studies that employ the term 'deliberate self-harm' often do so in ways which conflict with each other. Such inconsistencies in definition and specification of intention of acts further hamper efforts to build an overall accurate picture of research on self-injury. Most 'deliberate self-harm' studies concentrate on self-poisoning, a number are on attempted suicide, some include both self-poisoning and self-injury and some do not specify a particular method of self-harm (Hawton et al., 1998).

Many medical studies on 'deliberate self-harm' focus on the risk of suicide. According to this perspective, half of those who die by suicide have a history of 'deliberate self-harm'. Within the year following an episode of self-harm, the person is 100 times more likely to die by suicide than members of the general population (Cooper et al., 2005). According to a UK research on young people, teenagers self-injure twice as much as they self-poison (Hawton et al., 2002). However, 90 per cent of hospital Accident and Emergency referrals for 'deliberate self-harm' are due to self-poisoning and most of the remaining 10 per cent due to self-injury such as cutting (Hawton and James, 2005; Hurry, 2000). And as Hurry remarked in her study, the 10 per cent who cut themselves, usually do so 'without serious risk to life' (31). The amalgamation of self-poisoning and self-injury under the one term of 'deliberate self-harm' means that self-injury is more likely to be deemed a suicidal behaviour than it perhaps is (Thomas, 1998).

In relation to definitions of self-injury as the topic of this study (informed by research with people who self-injure), absence of suicidal ideation is essential. When people are asked to explain their self-injury, they often give meanings that are in direct opposition to theories of suicide (Adler and Adler, 2007, 2011; Arnold, 1995; Bristol Crisis Service for Women, 2000; Babiker and Arnold, 1997; Pembroke, 1994). The importance of the anti-suicide meaning is also emphasised in publications which offer support, advice and information for those who self-injure, their families and friends, professionals and anyone who is interested in learning about self-injury: 'Whatever similarities self-injury may bear to suicidal acts, it is not about dying. Rather it is about trying to cope and carry on with life' (Bristol Crisis Service for Women, 2000). People who self-injure do so for a number of reasons, which are more to do with life-preservation than about life-ending, chiefly, reduction of negative emotion or relief from psychological numbness. Walsh (2008) makes nine points of difference between self-injurious acts and acts which are suicidal. These include important distinctions in intention, level of damage and method used. According to this author, a person who is suicidal wishes to end psychological distress by ending consciousness whereas the intention behind self-injury is the relief of psychological distress. Methods used in suicide attempts are often highly lethal, for example, hanging or severing a main artery. In contrast, an act of self-injury usually carries low lethality, for example, superficial cuts to flesh on arms or legs (Walsh, 2008). It is also important to note here that the distinction between suicide and self-injury can appear blurred as many individuals who self-injure do feel suicidal at times (e.g. Whitlock et al., 2006a; Muehlenkamp and Gutierrez, 2004; Nock et al., 2006; Hawton et al., 2000). However, there are clear and important differences between occasions when they self-injure to alter their psychological state (as in self-injury) and occasions when they wish to end consciousness completely (suicide). Moreover, an important consequence of confusing self-injury with suicide when it is not is that self-injury may be viewed as an attempt to control and/or to manipulate others (Babiker and Arnold, 1997). These and other social costs to individuals who self-injure will be discussed in detail in Chapter 6.

For the purposes of this study, self-injury is defined as the non-suicidal and culturally unacceptable infliction of injury and/or pain to the self. Often people who self-injure will do so by cutting their arms, sometimes their hands, legs and abdomen as well as other less commonly used parts of the body, such as the face and genitals. In addition to cutting, people may burn, hit, scald and pinch, bang themselves off hard surfaces and pick at wounds.

Who self-injures?

Most self-injury is carried out in private, often without the knowledge of family members and friends. Its secretiveness therefore makes it extremely difficult to estimate the extent of self-injury in the general population and to notice groups of people who might be particularly affected. Definitional problems as to what is, or is not, regarded as self-injury and its conflation with suicide as discussed above, prove a major obstacle in the construction of an accurate statistical estimation of the phenomenon (especially in the UK). Moreover, even if definitional issues were addressed, approximations derived from medical studies usually remain inferentially restricted to populations of individuals who are known to, and are being treated by, medical authorities. As a result, a lot of what we know about self-injury is based on self-injuring people who are deemed mentally ill (e.g. Alderman, 1997; Deiter et al., 2000; Linehan, 1993), and/or are mandatory residents of institutions such as prisons (Haines and Williams, 1997; Melzer et al., 1999). The difficult task of what lies ahead is to discuss who self-injures and why. Some of the main groups of people associated with self-injury are presented, beginning with demographic factors relating to the general population, age and gender. Then we look at what the dominant medical perspective (such as categorisations and diagnoses; organic and psychological factors; and psychosocial 'risk factors') can tell us about the behaviour and the people who practise it. Focus then shifts to some of the studies addressing the perspectives of people who self-injure. Following on, this chapter gives a brief introduction (to be discussed further in Chapter 9) to the emergence of a new self-injuring population of people who do not seem to fit traditional psychological stereotypes. Finally, a summary of theoretical approaches to self-injury reveals some gaps in how it can be understood and how the study upon which this book is based has attempted to fill them.

Self-injury and the general population

Prevalence of self-injury in the general population seems to be on the increase. Estimations have grown since the early 1980s when 400 per 100,000 in population were thought to be deliberate self-harming (Pattison and Kahan, 1983) to 1000 per 100,000 in population (Favazza, 1998). Possible influences in this 150 per cent rise in a 20-year period could be attributed to greater public awareness of self-injury and more accurate reporting (Walsh, 2008). Alternative explanations for the rise have been attributed to an increased willingness among people who self-injure to disclose their self-injury and greater social tolerance towards the behaviour (Tantam and Huband, 2009).

A few non-clinical studies have been carried out. However, there remains a 'hidden population' of people who self-injure. Individuals in this group are not known to health establishments. They do not seek medical attention in relation to self-injury or related issues and therefore do not appear in medical statistics (Hurry, 2000; Smith et al., 1998; Tantam and Whittaker, 1992). In a survey of 37 women who had self-injured repeatedly, 9 reported never having been to Accident and Emergency departments in relation to the behaviour (Sutton, 1999).

As far as the issues of race and class are concerned, the few studies that do exist highlighting these aspects of self-injury tend to be conflicting. Regarding race, one argument favours self-injury as being a predominantly Caucasian phenomenon (Bhugra et al., 2002). The other claims high rates among minority groups (Adler and Adler, 2001; Marshall and Yazdani, 1999; Whitlock et al., 2006a). People who self-injure come from all walks of life. According to Strong (1998:18), the people interviewed in her book included 'doctors and lawyers, nurses and Sunday-school teachers, artists, singers and poets, teenagers and grandparents'. Similarities between self-injury and eating disorders have also contributed in the past to suppositions that self-injury is a particular affliction of middle and upper classes (Strong, 1998), assumptions which have not so far been supported in research. In fact, according to Whitlock (2010), writing for Cornell

University's Research Programme on self-injurious behaviour, the relationship between self-injury and trauma tends to support the speculation that low-income individuals are likely to be affected.

Self-injury and age

When studies are age-restricted to young people, higher rates of self-injury are reported. For example, two surveys of high school students reported that between 14 and 15 per cent had self-injured (Laye-Gindhu and Schonert-Reichl, 2005; Ross and Heath, 2002). Although self-injury can begin in childhood, its typical onset is more often between 12 and 14 years of age (e.g. Arnold, 1995; Favazza and Conterio, 1989; Herpertz, 1995; Nock et al., 2006). Studies of college students have reported that between 30 and 40 per cent of respondents initiate self-injury at the age of 17 or later and many continue using self-injury for periods of five years and more (Whitlock, 2006a). It would appear that although self-injury can begin or continue into later life, it is more likely to affect young people. However, this portrayal may also have something to do with teenagers having 'greater visibility and communication' than older people (Adler and Adler, 2011:33). Nevertheless, there is little information on self-injury specific to older people. Babiker and Arnold (1997) suggest that higher rates for self-injury in lower age groups is perhaps due to a number of age-related issues affecting youth. These may include factors such as still being under significant influence of adults who may be inadequately supportive or abusive; lack of power, control and choice; bullying; and identity issues such as sexuality. These authors suggest that the apparent reduction of self-injury with age could be due to greater emotional maturity. Older people may be more able to discard 'the oppressive role expectations which beset them when younger' (Babiker and Arnold, 1997:45). They also note however that unreported self-injury in older people may also be a relevant factor in the relatively low appearance of this group in research (1997). Furthermore, Tantam and Huband (2009:6) suggest that among older people who do hurt themselves in this way, 'the shame associated with self-injury is felt more keenly as one grows older'.

In addition to youth in general, young people who are receiving treatment for mental health issues seem to be at an even higher risk of self-injury than the general population. Briere and Gill (1998) reported levels of self-injury in both clinical and non-clinical populations of adults as 21 and 4 per cent, respectively. When youth and clinical populations are taken together, the rate of self-injury rises dramatically to between 40 per cent and 80 per cent in adolescent psychiatric patients (Darche, 1990; Nock and Prinstein, 2004).

Self-injury and gender

Both sexes self-injure, although there is a commonly held assertion that more women than men are affected (e.g. Hawton et al., 2006; Laye-Gindhu and Schonert-Reichl, 2005; Ross and Heath, 2002; Whitlock et al., 2006a). In the late 1990s, literature reporting women as outnumbering men varied widely in degrees of ratio, from 2:1 women to men, up to 20:1 (Babiker and Arnold, 1997). Over the past few years, however, some conflicting reports have cited men as being equally as likely to self-injure as women, particularly those which have been based on non-clinical samples (Garrison et al., 1993; Gratz, 2001; Klonsky et al., 2003; Muehlenkamp and Gutierrez, 2004). Research carried out in Accident and Emergency departments in the United Kingdom reported men as outnumbering women by more than half (Hawton and Catalan, 1987; Robinson and Duffy, 1989). Large disparities in gender ratios could be a reflection of inconsistencies in definitions, especially in the United Kingdom. Hawton (2000), who includes self-poisoning in his criteria for 'deliberate self-harm', reported a low ratio of 1.2:1 women to men. Studies which restrict definitions to self-injury only suggest that gender differences may be accounted for by the method used. Men are more likely to burn or hit themselves whereas women cut (Claes et al., 2007; Laye-Gindhu and Schonert-Reichl, 2005). For authors who report higher rates of self-injury in women, explanations of socialisation are given. Women are expected to internalise, and men to externalise, anger (Babiker and Arnold, 1997; Miller, 1994; Smith et al., 1998). This supposition is strengthened by studies of self-injury in groups of individuals who would be considered somewhat powerless in society, such as psychiatric inpatients and prisoners (Bristol Crisis Service for Women, 2000; Burstow, 1992; Smith et al., 1998). Similarly, as with the possibility that self-injury is likely to remain unreported in older people, men may be reluctant to seek medical attention regarding their self-injury or take part in research. They may also feel the behaviour is more stigmatising for them than for women and may be more likely to pass their self-injury off as accidental (Jayloe,

2003). However as women also hide injuries and pass them off as the results of accidents (Hodgson, 2004), it is difficult to say with much certainty. It is important to mention here also that the typical demographic profile of self-injuring individuals is being challenged. Adler and Adler's (2011) recent publication asserts that self-injury has followed eating disorders as a phenomenon which was initially believed to affect mostly Caucasian, middle class females, to increasingly being visible in other demographic groups. Males of all ages, non-white ethnicities and people from lower socioeconomic statuses are more and more associated with self-injury. Interestingly, as they also point out, these are groups which 'suffer from structural disadvantages in society' (2011:37).

The medical perspective

Categorisations and diagnoses

Influenced by structuralism, the standard medical approach to a problem of abnormal behaviour is to assign it to a category in accordance with the main diagnostic tools in psychiatry: the American Psychiatric Association's Diagnostic and Statistical Manual of Mental Disorders (4th ed., TR) (2000) and the World Health Organisation's International Classification of Diseases (ICD-10) (2007). Under these classification systems, self-injury is viewed not as an illness itself, but as a symptom of a number of underlying disorders 'most notably those having to do with impulse control' (Adler and Adler, 2007: 539). Calls have been made for self-injury to be recognised as a distinct diagnosis rather than a symptom (Alderman, 1997; Favazza and Rosenthal, 1993; Pattison and Kahan, 1983). Although the most common diagnosis given (both in the USA and the UK) is borderline personality disorder (Klonsky et al., 2003; Klonsky and Muehlenkamp, 2007; Leibenluft et al., 1987; Martinson, 1998; Schaffer et al., 1982; Walsh and Rosen, 1988), self-injury is held as symptomatic of several other underlying illnesses. Anxiety and depressive disorders are also correlated with self-injury (Andover et al., 2005; Klonsky et al., 2003; Klonsky and Muehlenkamp, 2007; Ross and Heath, 2002). Other related disorders include eating disorders (Favazza et al., 1989; Klonsky and Muehlenkamp, 2007) and substance disorders, such as alcohol or drug abuse (Bowen and John, 2001; Klonsky and Muehlenkamp, 2007; Langbehn and Pfohl, 1993). Individuals may also be diagnosed with more than one psychiatric disorder (Isacsson and Rich, 2001). Klonsky and Muehlenkamp (2007) have pointed to a number of shared psychological characteristics (to be discussed below) which have been identified in both individuals who self-injure and people with psychiatric disorders.

In the case of borderline personality disorder, the diagnosis is often given on the basis of the self-injurious behaviour alone (Martinson, 1998). This author does not imply that the disorder is a fictional illness. She does however go on to highlight extreme consequences of a misdiagnosis of borderline personality disorder, such as individuals being 'frequently treated as outcasts by psychiatrists' (Martinson, 1998). A 'borderline' stereotype can lead to a stigma being attached to the behaviour and punitive treatment from medical staff (Babiker and Arnold, 1997; Johnstone, 1997; Pembroke, 1994). Strong (1998) and Johnstone (1997) have also noted a sexist element to this diagnosis, as it is disproportionately applied to women. In addition, it is argued that the label is a pseudo-explanation based on a circular argument:

> Why does a woman cut herself? Because she has a borderline personality disorder. How do you know she has a personality disorder? Because she cuts herself. (Johnstone, 1997:422)

The unhelpfulness, in many cases, of the diagnosis of borderline personality disorder, attributing unwanted behaviour to abnormal personalities, additionally allows professionals to cease investigations into other possible origins of self-harming behaviour (Babiker and Arnold, 1997; Johnstone, 1997; Tantam and Whittaker, 1992). Moreover, the categorisation is inclined to deflect interest away from helping the individual, and may even result in the denial of assistance (NICE, 2004). The medical model positing self-injury as a symptom of underlying psychiatric problems has dominated discussions on the behaviour and has been reinforced by insufficient empirical evidence from non-clinical samples. Attempts to redress this imbalance have begun in recent years with increasing research into self-injuring populations of young people, college and general populations (e.g. Adler and Adler, 2007, 2011; Hodgson, 2004; Kokaliari, 2004; Whitlock et al., 2006a).

Biological factors

Theories relating to organic causes of unwanted behaviours and mental disorders/illnesses are a focus of this medical approach. For example, abnormalities in levels of the chemical serotonin in the brain have been associated with self-injury (Dallam, 1997; Simeon et al., 1992). It has also been suggested that the release of endorphin chemicals brought on by self-injury may be related to addictive characteristics of the behaviour (Pies and Popli, 1995) as many people who self-injure express the urge to hurt themselves even when no apparent trigger is present. These endogenous opiods are experienced as pleasant and are linked to relief from psychological distress. Withdrawal responses can lead to further self-injury (Grossman and Siever, 2001). These authors have also put forward a pain hypothesis which suggests self-injury as a means to end episodes of dissociation (Grossman and Siever, 2001) experienced by many people who self-injure.

Psychological characteristics

People who are in contact with medical services in relation to self-injury are reported to possess and exhibit more negative psychological characteristics than those who are not. According to Klonsky and Muehlenkamp (2007:1047): 'Self-injurers have been found to score highly on measures of negative temperament, emotion dysregulation, depression, and anxiety (e.g. Andover et al., 2005; Gratz and Roemer, 2004; Klonsky et al., 2003)'. Such negative and uncontrolled emotions are relieved on a temporary basis by the actions of self-injury (Klonsky, 2007; Klonsky and Muehlenkamp, 2007). In addition, Klonsky and Muehlenkamp (2007:1048) have pointed out that 'the link between borderline personality disorder and self-injury is not surprising because both have negative emotionality and emotion dysregulation as core features'.

  Problems with feeling detached from ones' experiences (medically termed 'dissociation') are associated with people who self-injure (Gratz et al., 2002; Zlotnick et al., 1996). They may also struggle to recognise or understand the meaning of emotions (Lundh et al., 2007; Zlotnick et al., 1996). From this perspective, people who self-injure are also viewed as poorly equipped in relation to their ability to understand and express their own emotions (Klonsky and Muehlenkamp, 2007).

As well as the above difficulties regarding emotions, self-injury is often associated with the traits of self-criticism and self-punishment (Herpertz et al., 1997; Klonsky et al., 2003; Soloff et al., 1994) and lately, to low self-esteem (Lundh et al., 2007). In addition, Klonsky and Muehlenkamp (2007:1048) argue that 'individuals high in both negative emotionality and self-derogation are at particular risk for self-injury, although research has not yet explicitly addressed the combination of these characteristics in relation to self-injury'.

Psychosocial 'risk factors'

Whilst the existence of an underlying illness is viewed as the root of self-injury, this perspective also recognises the importance of a number of social issues associated with the behaviour. These are often referred to as psychosocial 'risk' factors that affect the onset of self-injury in certain predisposed individuals. One of the main 'risk' factors concerns the importance of childhood experiences. There has been a great deal of research focusing on the link between sexual and physical abuse in childhood, and self-injury in later life (e.g. Briere and Gill, 1998; Gratz et al., 2002; Van der Kolk et al., 1991; Zoroglu et al., 2003). Additionally, abuse which has occurred early in life and been severe or prolonged is associated with increased dissociation and therefore greater self-injury (Brodsky et al., 1995). Klonsky and Muehlenkamp (2007), however, caution against taking for granted that people who self-injure have been abused. They add 'although child abuse may play an important role for some people's self-injury, many who have been abused do not go on to self-injure, and many who self-injure have not been abused' (Klonsky and Muehlenkamp, 2007:1049).

As well as overt abuse of a sexual and physical nature, there is literature which points to evidence of other less direct forms of abuse, especially those associated with caregiving relationships in childhood (e.g. Gratz, 2006; Green, 1978; Suyemoto and MacDonald, 1995; Tantam and Whittaker, 1992; Van der Kolk et al., 1991). According to Gratz (2006):

> [the] literature suggests the role of pathological family relationships, parent-child discord, and disrupted bonding in the risk of self-harm, highlighting both the importance of the context in which acts of abuse occur, as well as the fact that even among

individuals with no history of abuse, aspects of the parent-child relationship may have important consequences for adjustment (thereby possibly affecting the risk of later self-harm). (239)

Sexual and physical abuse are both 'strongly correlated' with 'self-destructive behaviour in adulthood' (Van der Kolk et al., 1991). However in summarising their findings these authors conclude that:

> neglect [is] the most powerful predictor of self-destructive behaviour. This implies that although childhood trauma contributes heavily to the initiation of self-destructive behaviour, lack of secure attachments maintain it. [Those] who had experienced prolonged separations from their primary caregivers, and those who could not remember feeling special or loved by anyone as children, were least able to…control their self-destructive behaviour. (Van der Kolk et al., 1991)

Many people it would seem, who have been abused in childhood, self-injure, although others have not (at least they have not revealed abuse in studies). Some scholars are identifying less obvious, but nonetheless negative childhood environments, which they have categorised under the umbrella term 'invalidating environments' (Gratz, 2006; Linehan, 1993). 'Invalidating environments' they assert, are influential factors in the development of borderline personality disorder (of which self-injury is often seen as a symptom) (Linehan, 1993) and self-injury (Gratz, 2006). 'Invalidating environments' are those in which the expression of one's personal encounters and perspectives is erroneously, excessively and inconsistently received. Communication of one's experiences is belittled, ignored or punished. Expressions of undesirable emotions are strongly discouraged, and significant others may be both excessively concerned and neglectful to one's needs (Gratz, 2006; Linehan, 1993). According to Linehan (1993), there are two basic features to invalidation. First, invalidated people are told that they are incorrect in both their accounts and understandings of their own experiences. And second, the individuals are blamed for any negative experiences that may befall them as a result of their own disagreeable attributes. It would seem then that sexual and physical abuse are seen as 'risk' factors in later self-injury. Moreover, whether sexually or physically abused or not, invalidation is regarded as a 'risk' factor in self-injury (Gratz, 2006).

The development (via quantitative medical studies) of a model for identifying 'high risk' individuals has been criticised regarding its overarching tendency to focus on statistical relationships between self-poisoning, suicide and self-harm, while lacking an interest in individual meanings attached to behaviour. The critics argue that 'moving beyond the identification of correlates towards effective treatment requires an understanding of the meaning and context of the act of self-injury itself, something which can only be gained by extensive interviewing of self-injurers' (Solomon and Farrand, 1996:112). However, because quantitative design is the mainstay of medical research, the perspective of the individual is usually stifled by the deductive nature of pre-structured methods. In addition, 'borderline personality' diagnoses influence the way in which the opinions of people who self-injure are received. Walsh and Rosen (1988), for example, argue that the views and explanations put forward by self-injuring individuals are unlikely to be reliable or accurate. They state:

> The intent of acts of self-harm is often a mystery to the perpetrators themselves. This intent may be unconscious, preconscious, or just muddled due to a rush of hopelessly confused thoughts and emotions... Other mutilators may provide explanations that were originally suggested to them by friends or professionals at previous points in time. Whether these 'explanations' resemble their own original intentions is unclear. (25)

Such comments may be viewed as undermining perspectives and removing 'ownership' of knowledge of self-injury from those who practise the behaviour.

Although the medical perspective, informed in the main by clinical samples derived from populations of self-injuring people attending accident and emergency and inpatient departments and outpatient clinics, remains the leading voice of authority on self-injury, a growing number of qualitative and non-clinical studies are increasingly promoting the perspective of the self-injuring individual.

Some perspectives of those who self-injure

The perspectives of people who self-injure in relation to causes and functions is most clearly demonstrated in a number of qualitative studies, carried out mainly by psychologists (Arnold, 1995; Harris, 2000; Marshall and Yazdani, 1999; Solomon and Farrand, 1996; Spandler, 1996) and a few sociologists (Adler and Adler, 2005, 2007, 2011; Hodgson, 2004). These authors would argue that the best way to find out about self-injury is to ask people who self-injure about their experiences. The 76 women who took part in Arnold's study offered 'considerable insights' into the behaviour (Arnold, 1995: 24). She was impressed by 'the depth of women's own understanding of their self-injury'. Qualitative research offering the perspectives of individuals who self-injure highlights the point that explanations of the behaviour vary from person to person, and that the point of view of each individual must be listened to. A number of themes to emerge from this perspective have been highlighted by both psychological and sociological scholars.

Perhaps the most constant theme agreed upon across individuals who take part in qualitative studies on self-injury is the role of past trauma (which has been discussed above). Smith et al. (1998) comment on the experiences of women who self-injure:

> there is a common factor in the lives of all women who self-harm. When talking about themselves and their experiences, they tell us that during their childhood years they have experienced trauma; physical abuse, sexual abuse, severe emotional abuse, repeated surgery and/or invasive medical treatment; and other forms of trauma such as witnessing violence. (21)

These authors go on to point out that not everyone who has experienced such trauma self-injures and stress the importance of psychological support for people in helping them recover from negative experiences:

> What seems to affect whether or not we do [self-injure], is whether or not the emotional care we received after that traumatic experience was appropriate. (Smith et al., 1998:22)

Learning to understand and to deal with painful emotions with the assistance of a significant other in childhood is essential if the individual is to be able to deal with periods of 'great emotional distress'. When invalidation (as previously discussed) of one's emotions and experiences is lacking, self-injury or other forms of self-harm are ways in which some people cope. These authors assert that behaviours which lead to 'borderline personality disorder' diagnoses are 'predictable and normal human responses to such trauma' (Smith et al., 1998:30).

Self-injury is a response to distressing events or environments. It can begin and be maintained for a number of reasons, with individuals feeling the need to express, make sense of, and cope with their circumstances by way of self-injury (Bristol Crisis Service for Women, 2000). Self-injurious acts can become highly functional for the individuals who practise the behaviour. Qualitative research has uncovered a number of positive functions provided by self-injury. The women who took part in Harris' (2000) study

> claimed that medical and nursing professionals viewed their self-harm as irrational and illogical. However a qualitative examination of the motivations and interests of all parties reveals that self-harm acts possess situated internal logic, whereas professionals tend to use rational logic in attempting to understand them. (2000:164)

The functions most likely to feature in these studies include: relief from emotional distress; distraction; self-punishment; communication; control and self-comfort; ending dissociation; and those relating to the symbolism of blood.

- Relief from emotional distress: At the centre of explanations of those who have used self-injury is the presence of extreme emotional distress (Arnold, 1995, 2000; Babiker and Arnold, 1997; Harris, 2000; Marshall and Yazdani, 1999; Pembroke, 1994; Smith et al., 1998; Solomon and Farrand, 1996; Sutton, 1999). Smith et al. (1998:35) cite moods characterised by feelings such as 'self-loathing' and 'low self-esteem' precipitating emotions such as 'anxiety, agitation and anger', and including reasons as to why they should self-injure. Many have reported self-injury as a form of self-protection against more severe self-harm. Indeed emotional distress is often described as reaching such unbearable levels that self-injury becomes the preferable option to more serious self-harm or suicide (Babiker and Arnold, 1997; Pembroke, 1994). When emotional tension reaches intolerable levels, self-injury is a way to effect emotional release, relief and calm. This alleviation of inner turmoil is, however, only temporary, lasting for periods of time, varying from a few hours to weeks, with the need for further self-injury arising again (Smith et al., 1998; Sutton, 1999). Smith et al. (1998) state:

> This 'relief' is usually only temporary. Self-harming behaviour cannot remove the cause of the emotional pressure and so when anything happens that triggers negative feelings, and the level of arousal builds up, the woman will feel the need to self-harm again. In this way self-harm can become a cycle of behaviour. (Smith et al., 1998:36)

Sutton describes a pervading 'grief reaction' after incidents of self-injury, marked by guilt, shamefulness and self-repulsion.

- Distraction: As well as providing relief from unbearable emotional distress, self-injury also functions to distract the individual by replacing emotional pain with physical pain, and thereby making it more manageable (Babiker and Arnold, 1997; Solomon and Farrand, 1996; Spandler, 1996). Solomon and Farrand (1996) suggest a possible explanation as to why individuals prefer physical pain as more bearable than emotional pain: 'Its origins are obvious and unproblematic, whereas the origins of emotional distress may not only be unclear but also too difficult to face' (Solomon and Farrand, 1996:117). Babiker and Arnold (1997) make an interesting point also, regarding the functions of self-injury in contrast to other forms of self-harm such as alcohol and/or drug abuse. Distraction and relief from emotional pain is not only instant with self-injury, it also allows the individual to focus on other aspects of daily life such as work or school.

- Self-punishment: The theme of guilt is not only associated with how individuals feel after they self-injure. Feelings of guilt also often precipitate self-injurious acts. The motivation to self-injure as self-punishment can be associated with previous abuse (Spandler, 1996). They may feel they deserve to be punished for feeling unwanted emotions such as anger (Arnold, 2000; Babiker and Arnold, 1997; Smith et al., 1998). They may also adopt and internalise insinuations made by their abusers that they were deserving of, or even 'wanted' the traumatic events that they experienced leading them to feel 'bad' or 'evil' (Smith et al., 1998:38). In addition, these authors also came across women who used self-injury to punish themselves for becoming sexually stimulated during abusive encounters (Smith et al., 1998).

- Communication: It has been suggested that self-injury is a form of communication, on both personal and public levels. Some authors (usually from a medical perspective) view self-injury as a means to coerce others to provide attention, kindness and sympathy (e.g. Feldman, 1988; Klonsky and Muehlenkamp, 2007; Walsh and Rosen, 1988). Indeed, Klonsky and Muehlenkamp, (2007) suggest that:

> An individual might self-injure to elicit affection from a significant other or loved one or to elicit reinforcing responses from authority figures or peers in correctional, clinical or school settings... Some people may not be fully aware that their self-injury is encouraged or reinforced by its effects on others (Klonsky and Muehlenkamp, 2007:1050).

The implication that self-injury is an attempt to manipulate others is strongly rejected by many authors whose work is based on personal accounts of individuals who practise it (e.g. Arnold, 1994, Pembroke, 1994). However, it is also acknowledged that the behaviour may be an attempt to convey to others the seriousness of their inner suffering and distress when verbal explanations are out of reach (Bristol Crisis Service for Women, 2000; Babiker and Arnold, 1997; Burstow, 1992; Crowe and Bunclarke, 2000; McLane, 1996; Spandler, 1996). The doubtfulness of self-injury as a way to communicate to others is demonstrated by pervasive accounts of acts of self-injury carried out secretively (Smith et al., 1998; Solomon and Farrand, 1996). The more likely communicative function fulfilled by self-injury is one of self-communication (Babiker and Arnold, 1997; Harris, 2000; Solomon and Farrand,

1996). From this point of view, self-injury allows the individuals private communication with themselves:

> For many people who self-injure, horrible and traumatic past experiences have been denied, minimised or ignored. An individual may feel self-injury to be a form of testimony; a way of being true to themselves and honouring their own experience and resulting feelings. (Babiker and Arnold, 1997:79)

- Control and self-comfort: According to Alderman (1997), a perception of control is essential for our psychological and physical well-being:

> When we feel in control of our environment, we feel better. We are more confident, happier and even physically healthier when we have a sense of control. (Alderman, 1997:50)

Feelings of powerlessness are common expressions in personal accounts of people who self-injure (Babiker and Arnold, 1997). Self-injury enables the individual to gain a degree of control of lives in which they may not otherwise have much power. Self-injuring prisoners often cite a desire for control as a motive for harming themselves in the highly controlled prison environment (Babiker and Arnold, 1997).

Some theorists suggest that self-injury can be an attempt to understand and deal with previous and unresolved experiences of trauma, by reliving the experience (Babiker and Arnold, 1997; Miller, 1994; Smith et al., 1998). 'Trauma re-enactment', as referred to by Miller, is self-injury as a representation of past abuse (Miller, 1994). Re-enactment of abuse can be a way to exert some control over traumatic memories when little, if any, was possible during the original experience. In addition to using self-injury as a chance to control and comprehend memories of traumatic experiences, it can also offer a chance to self-comfort. According to Smith et al.:

> Often after an episode of self-harm, the skin is soothed and cared for. This comforting, needed to repair the damage, did not occur in response to the original trauma but in occurring in the present becomes a reparation for past failures. (1998:42)

- Ending dissociation: As well as expressions of the behaviour as a way to cope with unbearably high levels of distress, many individuals who self-injure report feeling a sense of numbness, deadness or depersonalization which can be quickly and reliably ended by cutting or burning themselves (Favazza and Conterio, 1989; Smith et al., 1998; Strong, 1998). Dissociation is often associated with childhood sexual abuse whereby the child psychologically 'switches off' from dangerous circumstances from which there is no escape, or assistance from others (Smith et al., 1998; Strong, 1998). According to Smith et al.:

> This is not a conscious act; it is the way in which our minds protect us from unbearable pain and terror. It is like a state of self-generated hypnosis. At a later time, triggers associated with this original trauma can unconsciously lead to a similar dissociative state. A dissociative state leaves a person with a feeling of deadness and disconnection from others. Many women talk about feeling 'cut off' as if they might 'just drift out of existence and never come back'.... (Smith et al., 1998:37)

Self-injury serves the function of ending dissociative states, by providing the body with a sudden and immediate 'jolt' which helps the individual to be reunited with his or her surroundings (Herman, 1992).

- Symbolism of blood: In contrast to other forms of self-harm, and self-injurious acts such as burning, the cutting of one's skin and the letting of blood has powerful symbolic functions for many people who self-injure (Babiker and Arnold, 1997; Crowe and Bunclarke, 2000; Solomon and Farrand, 1996; Sutton, 1999). Women in Sutton's (1999) research reported the effect of watching blood ooze or flow from a wound, as symbolic of suppressed emotions being released. Babiker and Arnold (1997:81) also reported functions of purification served by bleeding, such as 'cleansing', 'purging' and ridding oneself of 'badness'. For those who seek to end dissociation or periods of feeling 'dead', the sight of blood helps them to feel 'real', or in Klonsky and Muehlankamp's (2007:1050) terminology, the promotion of 'feeling generation'.

When the range of positive functions of self-injury uncovered in qualitative studies is heard, one can perhaps appreciate how the behaviour becomes a tried and tested means to cope with psychological distress. The overarching opinion regarding how self-injury is learned, from studies based on the experiences of people who self-injure, points to self-learning (Adler and Adler, 2007; Hodgson, 2004), as a result of accidents or spontaneously arising from extreme emotional distress:

> Most participants in my research said they had never heard of cutting before engaging in it, and some even thought they 'invented' it ... While accidents happen, and some participants got their start from an accidental injury, other individuals seem to start almost intentionally: One day they cut themselves and realised they felt better afterward. For whatever reason, the individual felt the need to hurt themselves, followed through with that impulse and ended up continuing the behaviour. (Hodgson, 2004:171)

Some recent sociological interest

Sociological interest in self-injury is still in its infancy. Over the past few years, in studies based on non-clinical samples of self-injuring people, sociologists have identified societal changes which are affecting the meanings of the behaviour. Influences of the media and the internet are changing ways in which people discover and maintain the behaviour. While Hodgson's (2004) study supports the majority opinion that self-injury is self-learned (two-thirds of her respondents had no previous knowledge of the behaviour), her findings point, in addition, to an increase in self-injury as being learned from, and supported by, other sources: 'About one third of my participants indicated that they had heard or knew someone who cut prior to their own cutting'. Sources of learning ranged 'from books [and] friends to the internet' (Hodgson, 2004:171–2). Adler and Adler's (2007) study supports this shift, both in regard to sources of learning and maintenance of the behaviour. They have identified learning sources of self-injury in shifting societal structures:

> Individuals have begun to 'discover' self-injury in new ways, moving beyond the self-invention of the behaviour so common before the 1990s. Psychologists consider self-injury a practice that emerges spontaneously in troubled individuals, yet we note the

more widespread social learning of self-injury that has been trans-mitted through the media, health, education, and peer group inter-action. The psychomedical disease model, postulated as universal, overlooks the way self-injurers use their customary and ordinary sociological decision-making processes. Self-injury incorporates individuals' social perceptions, interpretations, anticipations and evaluations to plan and project lines of action. (2007:559)

These authors point to Sutherland's (1939) differential association theory to argue that 'the way people learn deviant behaviour and the general needs and values that drive it are expressions of the same processes as all other learning, needs and values' (Adler and Adler, 2007:559). Additionally, this sociological approach posits that the recent societal influences on how self-injury is learned and main-tained points towards a hidden group of older, long-term self-injur-ing individuals who are doing so 'in isolation, possibly unaware that there are others like themselves or even that self-injury is a phenom-enon' (Adler and Adler, 2005, 2007).

The recent sociological input into the study of this topic has inves-tigated self-injury in relation to how it is viewed in society. Whatever the meanings are for the individual regarding causes, functions and learning, self-injury remains a socially unacceptable and therefore stigmatised behaviour. This approach has not only identified how individuals use techniques to minimise deviant identities (Hodgson, 2004), but has also identified how the social changes mentioned above are affecting the stigma of self-injury:

These changing social definitions have potentially profound implications on the lives of self-injurers. Mitigation of their social stigma has diminished self-injurers' rejection, isolation and alien-ation. (Adler and Adler, 2007:561)

Some people who self-injure are beginning to not only 'reject the stigma' of self-injury, they are also, according to Adler and Adler (2007), 'embracing' the behaviour as part of their lifestyle choices. Psychologists too are taking into account the effects of social influ-ences on self-injury. They are investigating the effect of internet self-injury sites on the individual and are cautiously welcoming their use. While 'online interactions' may 'provide essential support' for people who self-injure, 'they may also normalise and encourage' the behaviour (Whitlock et al., 2006b).

Theoretical considerations

So far we have identified three main theoretical standpoints in the study of self-injury. These standpoints can be classed as: the psycho-medical model; the psychosocial model; and the sociological model. The psycho-medical model of self-injury is dominated by psychiatrics who view self-injury as an 'abnormal' behaviour, and symptomatic of underlying organic pathology. This approach studies self-injury via mostly quantitative studies drawn from clinical populations. Scholars behind the psychosocial model of behaviours are psychologists and psychiatrists who place importance on the role of both psychological characteristics innate to the individual and the relationship between the individual and his or her environment. Theories of learning are favoured in the psychosocial approach to understanding behaviour. Functions provided by self-injury reinforce and maintain the behaviour. Research on self-injury from this perspective employs both quantitative and qualitative research designs using clinical and non-clinical populations. The recent sociological model of self-injury is in its infancy. Like scholars of the psychosocial perspective, sociologists also use learning theories to understand phenomena. However, despite this overlap in the theoretical standpoints, sociologists place greater importance on how societal factors shape behaviour. Sociologists have focused on the self-injury debate on two main areas. First, recent sociological research in non-clinical populations has uncovered other factors which seem to point to a much more diverse self-injuring community than has so far been presented in studies restricted to patients of psychiatry (Adler and Adler, 2007, 2011). Second, social structures in regard to medicine, the media and the internet influence the meanings of self-injury (Adler and Adler, 2007, 2011; Hodgson, 2004). To date, sociological inquiry into self-injury has employed qualitative research designs in non-clinical populations. This approach has opened the debate on how self-injury is viewed as deviant behaviour in society, how those who practise it are stigmatised and deal with their stigmatisation and how changes in societal structures are affecting the meanings of self-injury.

It is clear that reviewing the literature on self-injury is a difficult task, hampered by inconsistencies in definitions by various authors to describe a number of behaviours and intentions. The inclusion of self-injury under the umbrella term 'deliberate self-harm' has led to the conflation of self-injury with self-poisoning and suicide. In terms of demographics, self-injury seems to affect more women than men, more young people than old and more people in psychiatric populations, although these findings have been questioned. Approaches in medically related studies are concerned with questions as to why people self-injure and posit the behaviour as symptomatic of underlying pathology. Qualitative studies which focus on accounts of people who self-injure tend to posit the behaviour as a generally functional and non-suicidal response to psychological distress. Both medical perspectives and accounts of self-injuring individuals converge on the issue of trauma as a precipitating factor to self-injury.

There are gaps in self-injury research. There appears to be a lack of non-clinical, qualitative and sociological studies on self-injury. The theme of suffering is convincingly argued across both the perspectives of medical scholars and those studies that focus on the perspective of the individual. There are however, gaps in self-injury research. There appears to be a lack of non-clinical, qualitative and sociological studies on self-injury.

What is offered in the following chapters is a discussion based on a non-clinical, qualitative study of self-injury from the perspective of the individual. The theoretical framework used is three-pronged. First, suffering has been identified as a strong theme, both from the medical viewpoint and from the point of view of the individual. It has not however been explored using an empirically grounded theoretical conceptualisation. This book explores the theme of suffering framed by the concept of 'trajectory' (Riemann and Schuutze, 2005) which examines suffering in the life of the individual who self-injures, and takes into account the processes of feeling 'driven' by uncontrollable outer forces. Second, the concept of rituals is a new area in the study of self-injury and has been raised spontaneously in a pilot study prior to this work. The theme of 'ritual' is not strange to sociological enquiry. Durkheim (1971) studied rituals in relation to the functions of communal bonding and healing. Self-injury is generally a solitary ritual that serves many functions for the individual and will be investigated in depth. Similarities can be drawn between needle fixation among drug users (McBride et al., 2001; Pates, 2001) and blade fixation in self-injury rituals. Self-injury is costly to the individual especially in terms of stigma. There are also more indirect costs arising from the process of suffering, many of which leave a long-lasting legacy to be contended with. This book will deal with costs in both of these spheres, and will include the themes of stigma, relationship problems, social paralysis and vulnerability, conceptualised as 'trajectory transformations' (Riemann and Schütze, 2005). Sociological attention to self-injury is relatively new. Where it has been applied, it has used data gathered from qualitative interviews with non-clinical samples. The theme of self-injury in relation to the wider society has identified a number of interesting topics for investigation. These include how individuals who self-injure react to the stigmatisation of the behaviour. Changes in social structures such as the media and the internet have influenced how self-injury is learned and maintained, and also how levels of stigma have been reduced somewhat.

The study upon which this book has been based is an inquiry into the experiences of self-injuring people and the meanings held by them. This book examines the main themes uncovered in the endeavour. In the remaining chapters, the people who took part are introduced and the issues which arose in talking with them are focused on. These are: processes of suffering as experienced by people who self-injure; an investigation into rituals of self-injury and their significance in the maintenance of the behaviour; a more in-depth investigation into the stigma of self-injury than has so far been articulated; costs that affect the individual regarding the long-lasting legacy of suffering from which self-injury emerged; how some people have moved away from this way of coping and finally how the face of self-injury is changing under societal influences.

3
Meet the People who Self-injure

'Sharp sparkling blade' [by Jane]

The sharp sparkling blade
Summons my love for a moment
I reach with my hand, my hate
To slide it beautifully
Across pure unblemished skin
Then I watch
I scream inside myself
I watch the blood flow down my arm
I watch life run from me
I smile, I am real
I bleed
I hurt
You have no fucking idea who I am

I knew from the outset, when planning this book, that a deep understanding of self-injury from the perspective of people who self-injure would involve listening to their individual stories and hearing
what they had to say on issues important to them. Over a period of
several months I sat with tape recorder, pen and notepad while 25
people shared what were oftentimes intimate and deeply personal
experiences of self-injury and related issues. What I was not prepared
for was the sheer depth of intimacy and honesty with which they
entrusted their feelings, understandings, confusions and fears, and
the eloquence with which they were articulated. Interviews were
planned as semi-structured, based on a list of topics that I wished to

cover. However, I decided early on in the process that it was important for people to feel as free as possible to discuss what was important to them and in a manner in which they felt comfortable. My topic guide was often dispensed with as participants began to relate their experiences. A few of them had previously shared some of the information with other people such as counsellors or trusted friends. Some of those who had done so, however, commented that they had never gone into so much detail or as in-depth as they did in our conversations. Many revealed that this was the first time they had ever told their stories to anyone, because they never felt comfortable in doing so and/or because no one had ever expressed an interest in hearing about their experiences. Interviews were participant-led and they talked extensively about their experiences, especially when time was unrestricted and they felt in control of the conversation. As well as the information garnered from the interviews, three participants kept diaries of self-injury for a period of four months and a further three contributed selections of poetry written during periods of active self-injury. All of this wonderful material formed the basis for this book.

Finding people to take part was achieved in a number of ways. The most successful method of recruitment was advertisement. The request *'Please help me understand self-injury'* along with the prerequisite that people should be over the age of eighteen and have self-injured (e.g. by cutting or burning), either currently or in the past, was placed in a variety of Belfast newspapers and on posters positioned throughout the city. Other sources of recruitment were contacts in health and well-being organisations and word of mouth.

The participants

As mentioned earlier, much of what is known about self-injury comes from research on people in medical settings. There is a hidden population of people who have not made themselves known to medical and counselling authorities in relation to their self-injury. It was my deliberate intention to get as broad and diverse a sample of self-injuring people as possible and included: those who have presented themselves in a medical setting in relation to self-injury; those who have contacted voluntary counselling organisations; and importantly, people who have not previously made themselves known to professionals or organisations regarding their self-injury. These three groups may overlap to some extent, but this approach was deemed the more likely to generate wider perspectives of self-injury.

People who were interested in taking part contacted me by email, telephone or in the case of two participants, via a contact in a health and well-being organisation who arranged and facilitated the interviews in a private office of a mental health day centre. Participants were given explanations of the study and their expected role in both verbal and written forms so that informed consent could be obtained. They were thanked at the end of each interview and I texted them on their mobile telephones within a few hours of us parting company to again acknowledge my appreciation for the time and effort involved in taking part. Interestingly, I received texted replies from some people which contained further statements on issues or stories they had remembered and also on what taking part in the research meant to them.

The real names of all participants have been changed in order to maintain confidentiality. Anonymity was assured under pseudonyms which were either chosen by participants for themselves or assigned by me. Interviews varied in length from one and a half hours to four hours. Most lasted about two and half hours on average. A choice of interview settings was offered to participants. Most chose to speak to me in my home, some in their home and the remaining few were interviewed in a mental health day centre or a private office in a workplace.

The people who took part in the study ranged in age between 19 and 44 years. They included students, a university researcher, a lab technician, an ex-teacher, a social worker, an ex-soldier, an office clerk, a clergyman and a community volunteer. Some were not in paid employment, but worked in the home looking after young children. Others were unemployed. They were 20 women and 5 men. The ratio of women to men reflects research on self-injury which suggests a gender bias in the behaviour. However, it should be noted that men may also be less willing to take part in research or to discuss such a delicate topic as self-injury (Babiker and Arnold, 1997). Most began self-injuring between the ages of 11 and 14 years. At the time of interviews (carried out between September 2005 and April 2006), about two-thirds of the people were regularly self-injuring. The rest had not self-injured for periods of months or years.

Over half of the participants revealed during the interviews that they had been sexually abused in childhood. Many were additionally physically abused. Mike, for example, a 40-year-old clergyman had suffered sexual abuse at the hands of three separate family friends. He began self-injuring at the age of 14 by dropping books onto his face until he bled as he lay on his bed. He progressed to cutting with knives and punching himself. For Mike, self-injury 'was a way of expressing... Trying to put out... An outward form of the interior agony that was going on'. In common with many people who self-injure it was also a way of ending periods of dissociation which he described as 'periods of total disembodiment... To inflict pain on yourself is like a way to bring you back into the world'.

As well as those who were sexually and physically abused in childhood, most of the people who took part in this book suffered invalidating environments as children and young people, usually from adults in caregiving roles. Jane, for example, was a 23-year-old, single and unemployed woman. She described growing up in a highly controlled and invalidating home environment and considered herself to be 'a very sensitive child'. She was bullied at school and began cutting with blades and knives at the age of eleven as a way to cope: 'When I cut I can think straight and carry on'. 'It feels natural to me... as natural as eating my breakfast feels natural'. Table 3.1 gives some basic facts about each person who took part. Additional information on participants is available in the Appendix (Pen-portraits of participants).

I asked the people who agreed to talk to me about their self-injury and those who kept a diary or contributed poetry, why they did so. Two main reasons for taking part in the research emerged. First, they hoped that they would benefit personally by telling their own individual story of self-injury and second, that others would gain from reading about their experiences. Tina, for example (a 39-year-old pre-school assistant), was motivated by a desire to increase her own understanding of her relationship with self-injury: 'Well I thought that talking to you about my self-injury might help me to figure it out a bit better myself'. She also, in common with many who took part, revealed that this was the first time she had told anyone about her self-injury in the context of her life story and the first time anyone had ever 'really listened' to her. The secretiveness of self-injury, due in no small part to the stigma attached to the behaviour, means

Table 3.1 Summary of participant information

Name	Age at interview (in years)	Age at first SI (in years)	Marital status	Employed	Trauma
John	39	18	Married	Yes	Emotional
Jane	23	11	Single	No	Emotional
Anne	19	14	Co-habiting	Student	Sexual, emotional
Kathy	30	16	Single	Stay at home parent	Physical, emotional
Nikea	27	13	Married	Stay at home parent	Physical, emotional
Susan	44	40	Married	Stay at home parent	Emotional
Tracey	39	14	Single	No	Sexual, physical, emotional
Nora	30	26	Single	Yes	Physical, emotional
Eve	38	31	Divorced	Stay at home parent	Emotional
Marie	27	14	Married	No	Sexual, emotional
Dawn	21	15	In relationship	Student	Physical, emotional
Tom	23	11	Single	Yes	Emotional
Rachel	26	18	Married	Yes	Emotional
Lena	28	14	Single	No	Sexual, physical, emotional
Steve	40	14	Divorced	No	Sexual, physical, emotional
Lisa	28	11	Single	No	Sexual, emotional
Laura	19	15	Single	No	Sexual, emotional
Ella	39	31	Divorced	No	Sexual, physical, emotional
Sally	34	11	Single	No	Sexual, emotional
Mike	40	14	Single	Yes	Sexual, emotional
Sam	42	12	Married	Yes	Sexual, physical, emotional
Tina	39	15	Married	Yes	Physical, emotional
Aoife	28	13	Divorced (in relationship)	Yes	Sexual, physical, emotional
Molly	32	12	Single	Yes	Sexual, physical, emotional
Deirdre	38	12	Married	Yes	Sexual, physical, emotional

Source: Pen-pictures of self-injury participants (Appendix)

that many people who self-injure feel isolated. Sam (a 42-year-old married sales assistant) gave this as a reason for taking part in the study:

> I always felt totally alone regarding my self-harm, especially when I was a teenager. I thought no other person on the planet cut themselves to feel better and I thought I'd be locked up for sure if anyone found out about it. It's terrible to feel like you're some sort of freak. Hearing about other people just like me and also the possibility of inspiring other people who self-injure to know that they are not alone inspired me to talk to you like this. So you could say I'm helping myself and others at the same time by talking to you. [Sam]

Often participants were interested in finding out about how their stories fitted in with the wider study and what, if anything, they had in common with the other people who took part. Where this interest was shown, I was content at the end of the interviews to give an overview of the research to date. At this point, some people asked me if I could explain their self-injury, or even advise them on how they might stop the behaviour. On these occasions I stressed that my role was that of researcher not counsellor. I did however offer advocacy. As well as outlining the findings of the study, I provided contact details of counselling groups and recommended websites that provide information and support for people who self-injure. Participants commented that they were pleased to be involved in the study and often revealed that hearing about other people who self-injure made them feel less isolated, or in Aoife's words, 'like less of a nutcase'. Sally (a 34-year-old disabled woman who had been sexually abused by a family member) was active in her plight to change public opinions and stereotypes about self-injury and people who self-injure. She had given media interviews, spoken at self-harm conferences and was now taking part in my study. Sally gave similar reasons to the others for taking part. She also expressed a desire to change public perceptions of self-injury by talking about her reasons for cutting herself and also by comparing it to socially acceptable forms of coping:

> The taboo needs to be broken down. We are not freaks. We are not attention seeking and we are not trying to kill ourselves. When we do this [self-injure], it's our way of coping with stuff that

happened … We attempt to understand the teenager who binge drinks hoping to find the answer at the bottom of their bottle or just escape. But if a young person sits down in front of us and says 'I cut', we panic, we judge, we medicate. We even lock them up. [Sally]

In Chapter 7, the issue of taking part in research is discussed further in relation to redefining the stigma of self-injury and related issues. Whether reasons given for taking part were motivated to benefit themselves or the wider society, it became clear that participation was an empowering experience despite the fact that many were visibly distressed and emotional during interviews.

Self-injury is an issue laden with emotion and can conjure up feelings of anger, dread and fear. The prospect of participants becoming distressed was a reality of the study and over half became visibly upset when speaking about experiences which were painful to recount. When this happened, participants were reminded that they were in control of deciding whether to continue or not. They were given the opportunity to take a break in order to regain composure before resuming, or alternately, terminating the interview. Although some were embarrassed at their emotional state in the presence of a relative stranger, all were adamant that the interviews proceeded. They did so with the aid of paper handkerchiefs and cups of tea and coffee. Many remarked on a 'need' to tell their stories and commented on the therapeutic effect of the interviews. Rosenthal (2003) has emphasised the therapeutic dimension of biographical interviews in particular and Kenyon (1996) suggests it can actually aid the person to find direction in life. However, as Kenyon also points out, interviews which require delving into one's life story is not for everyone and it could be judged ethically inappropriate to assume that it is. Moreover, going into a piece of research under the blinkered presumption that the process can only be a liberating or enlightening experience for participants can be viewed as patronising and condescending. Interviews for this study were ultimately led by participants. In regards to the design of the study, it is clear that the depth of valuable information yielded could only have come from sitting down with people who self-injure and listening to what self-injury meant to them in the context of their life story.

4
The Role of Suffering

'Heart failure' [by Dawn]

Oddly, sickly it makes me feel special
Not sure if special is the right word
But it's all I can think of
This is what I don't tell
I don't do it for the reasons above
I think that just makes it continue on
I started because I was in pain and really, I swear
I still am
So often

It would be impossible to get through one's life without experiencing some suffering on both physical and emotional levels. Indeed, most would argue that a certain amount of suffering is essential for (1) the healthy development of one's ability to self-protect, (2) a well-adjusted character, (3) empathy for others and (4) an appreciation of life's pleasures. It is when suffering is extreme and/or prolonged, especially beginning in childhood as developmental processes are taking place, that self-injury can become a tried and reused response to one's environment. This chapter considers how some people who self-injure are affected by suffering. It theorises the phenomenon as part of a 'trajectory' of suffering (Riemann and Schütze, 2005; all references to Riemann and Schütze in this chapter are from their work in 2005) and, in so doing, offers an understanding of self-injury that has not been previously put forward. Using this conceptualisation, we explore how self-injury can be viewed as a way (or biological action scheme) to psychologically escape from, and/or control, the effects of life disorder. It aids the suffering individual in exercising a degree of autonomy in the face of overwhelming external forces, which can otherwise render him or her generally powerless (at least in the beginning).

Extreme suffering in the form of childhood maltreatment and subsequent self-injury is a main theme in much research both within and outside the medical perspective of self-injury. The role of suffering in relation to self-injury was widely reported in this study. Out of the 25 people who spoke to me, over half revealed that they had been sexually abused. Many reported physical and emotional abuse. Most, who had been sexually abused, had been so in addition to the other forms of abuse reported. However, one of the most interesting findings of the study revealed that whether sexually and/or physically abused or not, most people (24 out of the 25 participants) revealed childhoods in which they suffered invalidation from adults in caregiving roles.

'Trajectories' of suffering and self-injury

The term 'trajectory' was originally applied by Glaser and Strauss (Glaser and Strauss, 1968; Strauss and Glaser, 1970) to provide a theoretical framework dealing with the complicated relationships between the development of illness, attempts to manage it and the subsequent suffering and dying of the afflicted individual. Following on from the original use of this concept of trajectory in the study of chronic illness, Riemann and Schütze developed it as a substantial theory applicable in broader terms to the study of biographical suffering which resulted from disorderly life processes in general. According to these authors, this advancement of the concept goes further than previous interactionist lines of investigation, which focused on action. Prins, who used the trajectory concept in his study of the course of drug addiction, stated that 'the main symbolic interactionist premise [is] that the behaviour of individuals is guided by the active observation and selection of situations and social contexts. Such active determination, however, is not always the case ... ' (Prins, 1995:49). It is at this point that the concept of trajectory becomes particularly useful in the study of self-injury. It brings to the fore the significance of 'social processes of being driven and losing control over one's life circumstances' (Riemann and Schütze:111). From this perspective, a trajectory refers to 'disorderly processes of suffering in the life of a person' (115). It is:

> ...structured by conditional chains of events which one cannot avoid without high costs, constant breaks of expectations and a growing and irritating sense of loss of control over one's life circumstances. One feels that one is driven, that one can only react to 'outer forces' which one does not understand.... (Riemann and Schütze: 112)

Although this refinement of the trajectory concept was developed on the basis of detailed sequential and comparative analyses of autobiographical offhand narratives in the context of narrative interviews (Schütze, 1981), I believe it may be fruitfully employed in this study which uses a different methodology involving semi-structured interviews. The trajectory is characterised by the features summarised in Table 4.1.

Riemann and Schütze apply this model of a 'trajectory' to the suffering of immigrants and cancer patients, but make it clear that these

Table 4.1   Key characteristics of a 'trajectory' of suffering

- The individual is overwhelmed by unexpected events. These events are experienced as powerful external forces which (at least in the beginning) cannot be controlled.
- The individual feels driven and conditioned by powerful outer forces which he or she cannot understand and control.
- The sources and features of the external forces are, at least partially, unknown in the eyes of the sufferer.
- The person is trapped by disorders of orientation and loss of personal capacity for controlled action.
- This is accompanied by sensations of becoming strange to oneself and exploring one's strange inner territory.
- The person's ability to start, establish and organise social relationships is weakened. Ability to trust is compromised.
- The everyday life of the individual seems to begin to 'shrink', even during non-peak trajectory situations.
- There is an interplay between powerful external forces and the reactions of the person which reinforce the dynamics of disorganisation in her or his life.
- The process opens opportunities for systematic reflection on suffering and mobilising biographical work and creativity.

Source: Derived from Riemann and Schütze (119–21).

Table 4.2   Sequential organisation of biographical trajectory

---

- Build-up of trajectory potential
- Crossing the border from an intentional to a conditional state of mind
- Precarious new balance of everyday life
- Downward spin
- Breakdown of self-orientation
- Attempts at coming to terms with the trajectory
- Practical working upon or escaping the trajectory

Source: Riemann and Schütze (126–33).

basic features of a 'biographical trajectory' can be seen in any process of suffering and life disorder. As such, it can be readily applied to the study of self-injury as a way to conceptualise the progress of suffering experienced by people who self-injure. The participants in this study exemplify the general features of a trajectory as developed by the above authors. Riemann and Schütze further organise the basic features of the trajectory into a chronological order as illustrated in Table 4.2.

These authors further make it clear that the chronological unfolding of the trajectory process should not be understood as a rigid or 'blind' progression and that the appearance of 'deviations from the elementary trajectory script' (133) can also be identified.

In order to illustrate how processes of suffering affect those who self-injure, we will undertake a closer examination of three stories (Steve's, Ella's and Jane's) which, in relation to suffering, particularly reflect the general experiences of the 25 people who took part in this study. Steve (aged 40) was emotionally, physically and sexually abused in childhood. Ella (aged 39) was sexually abused as a child and Jane (aged 23) was bullied in school. In addition all three suffered emotional invalidation from significant others.

The beginning of the trajectory of suffering

I grew up always being treated as a total waste of space

Riemann and Schütze (126) refer to the 'build-up of trajectory potential' to illustrate how external dynamics can interact to begin a system of capturing and controlling a person, which may at first go unnoticed. Unaware of any potential threat, no plans to offset the danger can be made. Moreover, the actions of the person may indeed help to lay the foundations of the trajectory, as in the authors' illustration of a young French couple's plan to emigrate to America; a plan which helped the trajectory to take hold. In this study of self-injuring individuals, 24 out of 25 participants experienced invalidation and/or other types of maltreatment in childhood from adults in caregiving roles. For these children, the trajectory did not go through a 'warm-up' stage, rather, it was experienced from birth. The sense of morbid familiarity that surrounded their suffering meant that it was often not until a greater level of maturity and increased understanding of their situation was attained (usually around the age of eleven – which coincides with the age at which many individuals began to self-injure) that the full horror of their predicament was revealed to them.

The theme of childhood maltreatment is cited in self-injury literature (both medical and otherwise) as the most reliable environmental predictor of the behaviour (Van der Kolk et al., 1991). In this study, sexual abuse was reported by over half of the participants, as was physical abuse and neglect. However, although exposure to these traumatic experiences during childhood and adolescence was cited as the main reason for the beginning of self-injury for these individuals, another less obvious form of childhood maltreatment was reported by 24 out of the 25 participants. The most consistent negative childhood environment reported by all these participants, whether abused or not, was characterised by the more common experience of invalidation. Invalidating environments have been discussed in Chapter 2. In this study, to remind the reader, they refer to those relationships in which one's caregivers may be inconsistent in their over and under involvement. The expression of personal interpretations are depreciated, ignored and/or penalised, as are demonstrations of distress (Gratz, 2006; Linehan, 1993). Gratz indicated the need for research to be expanded in the direction of environmental risk factors other than the more extreme forms of abuse to include less obvious forms of invalidation such as 'emotional neglect, disrupted bonding and psychological control' (Gratz, 2006:239).

The concept of the self, from the perspective of symbolic interactionism, is helpful at this point. From the moment we are born, we begin to develop a sense of self through a process of socialisation into society (Mead, 1934). According to Mead, there are two aspects to the self; the 'I' (myself as I am and the source of action) which is continually interacting with the 'me' (myself as a social self, reflecting how others see me) especially during role play with other children and in relationships with significant adults. By seeing how other people react to the world around them, children can construct their own sense of self. This allows the development of their moral conscience and they gradually take on widely held values and norms over two broad phases (Mead, 1934). Mead observed that:

> ...there are two general stages in the full development of the self. At the first of these stages, the individual's self is constituted simply by an organisation of the particular attitudes of other individuals toward himself and toward one another in the specific social acts in which he participates with them. But at the second stage in the full development of the individual's self, that self is constituted not only by an organisation of these particular individual attitudes, but also by an organisation of the social attitudes of the generalised other or the social group as a whole to which he belongs. (1934:163)

High dependence on judgements and feedback from others means, however, that the self is liable to be damaged when things go awry in the developmental period – a happening not fully explored by symbolic interactionist theorists of the developing self. One such liability according to Harter (1999) is concerned with:

> ...the internalisation of unfavourable evaluations of the self by others. The incorporation of the disapproving opinions of significant others will lead, in turn, to perceptions of personal inadequacy and to low self-esteem. (1999:6)

Similarly, in this study, the majority of participants had experienced negative attitudes from those in caretaking roles. It is therefore reasonable to assert that the selves of many of this study's participants had been damaged during the critical formation period. Their childhoods were characterised by exposure to invalidation, whether or not they were also more obviously abusive. These individuals, in other words, were born into trajectories of suffering.

Jane, Steve and Ella's trajectories of suffering began in early childhood and were experienced as powerful and uncontrollable external forces of invalidation and/or abuse in varying degrees, originating from adults in caregiving roles. Having been born into their trajectories of maltreatment, all three participants experienced the beginning of their suffering not as sudden intrusions on their lives, but as containing elements of an all-powerful 'normality', which could neither be understood nor controlled. Internalisation of unfavourable opinions of themselves from significant others led to the inevitable formation of damaged selves, characterised in particular by dominant low self-esteem. Let us begin with Jane, a 26-year-old mature student. Jane reported being neither abused nor traumatised during her early years but that her childhood was unpleasant nonetheless, especially in regard to her relationship with her mother:

> I had a troubled childhood but I wasn't abused or anything like that. It was strange...I had a difficult relationship with my mother...We weren't very close. She found it really difficult to communicate towards me...I felt like I was always trying to make my mum better. [Jane]

Her mother, according to Jane, suffered from depression and had frequent mood swings, which she 'took out' on Jane and her younger brother. Jane was not permitted to express unpleasant emotions, in particular anger, resulting in the internalisation of these feelings. Steve (40-year-old ex-soldier) and Ella (39-year-old single parent), in comparison to Jane, were born into more obvious trajectories of suffering. Steve, the youngest of five children, sums up his feelings of childhood as growing up and 'always being treated as a total waste of space'. He was placed in a residential children's care home at the age of five years as a result of his parents' apparent inability to take care of him and his older siblings. His vague early memories prior to this age were of alcoholic parents and a physically and emotionally abusive home life:

> My mum was an alcoholic...My mum was a loose woman. My father and her would knock the crap out of each other from what I remember of being there. [Steve]

When asked to tell me about self-injury in the context of his life story, Steve began by recounting the suffering endured as a young child in institutional care:

> Um ... Where do I start ... I think ... Late sixties, early seventies I was put in Riverview House Home. I was five years old ... I remember going into this mansion house ... Mrs Worthington was the matron there. It was run by the Church ... Um ... it was also funded by social services. I remember going to Church every Sunday and we were being talked about in Church by the Minister ... how we were children of loose women and alcoholics and the rest of the congregation loved to look down on us ... And we were always being marched about the town in small groups and everybody knew who we were. And we went to shops to help people with their shopping to raise money for the home. And I was in the home for so long ... And everyone knew who my mother and father were ... And still to this day 'You were in the home' .... The friends I made there ... We have an unspoken way that we communicate ... I mean a friend who wasn't in the home said 'You lot have a way of looking at each other when we are talking. Your eyes all dart about to each other like you are telepathic or when there's something that you all don't want to talk about ... like you all know something. What happened there anyway?' Well it was mental and physical abuse which stemmed from Mrs Worthington. We were tortured ... Always being thumped for nothing ... Always being punished for nothing. ... [Steve]

The incorporation of unfavourable opinions of himself, beginning in his home environment, was further reinforced in a statutory residential setting at the hands of an abusive matron and perhaps, less obviously, by his own internalisation of the perceived opinions of himself as viewed by the local community.

Similarly, Ella began her story by telling of the sexual abuse she suffered, from an extremely young age, at the hands of her father, and of the flashbacks she endured at the time of the interview as a 39-year-old woman:

> Well, from the age of three I was sexually abused by my father. It went on until I was sixteen. He's dead now thank God. He's been

dead for the past 22 years. I could be sitting quite calmly, doing nothing and it would happen. Or I would be out in the street and anything could bring it back. I would take flashbacks…. [Ella]

It is highly likely that all three participants' senses of self were severely damaged. In the early stages of the trajectory, 'the sources and features of the powerful outer forces are at least partially unknown' (Riemann and Schütze: 119). It was impossible for Jane, Steve and Ella to understand or conceptualise what was happening to them at such early ages. In retrospect, childhood memories are characterised by what Riemann and Schütze term 'an all-penetrating sense of fate and a generalised feeling of uncertainty', which seemed to darken their 'life horizons' (119).

Early action schemes

If I was a really good girl, Mum wouldn't be angry

Riemann and Schütze (128) refer to attempts to create a 'precarious balance' of 'everyday life', whereby the individual 'hyper-focuses on certain means for re-establishing a mental equilibrium'. Although study participants recounted childhoods fraught with confusion, fear and anxiety, they managed to cultivate various 'survival' techniques that they utilised in endeavours to stabilise their emotional integrity and lessen their day-to-day suffering. Steve lived in the residential home until he was ten years old when he went to live with his father and his father's second wife. However, the trajectory of emotional and physical abuse was set to continue at the hands of his stepmother and father. Although the source of Steve's maltreatment was experienced as overpowering and controlling, it is still possible to identify early attempts by Steve to take, what Riemann and Schütze (121) term, 'biographical action schemes for controlling the dynamics of disorder'.

And then I had left the home and went back to my father and stepmother for a time when I was about ten. It started with weekend visits which we thought was great at the time. But my stepmother systematically mentally and physically abused me. I was beat every other day…. My stepmother used to bake scones and at the end of the dough…. There's not enough to make two but you could make one big one. And when I got in from school she asked me if I would like one and to take one. Of course me being me I went for the biggest one and she slapped me round the head and said 'You're one greedy bastard! Out of all them you had to pick the biggest one'. That was her opportunity to tell me how bad I was and 'Your mother was a whore!' and to rant on. And then when my father came in from work…. By the time she had explained what had happened according to her he battered me as well…. Then the next time, maybe a month later when she was doing the scones again and she said 'Do you want a scone?' Of course I deliberately picked a fairly small one. And she said 'And what is wrong with the biggest one today? Is the biggest one not good enough for you today? You're one ungrateful bastard!' And the whole thing would start again. And then maybe a third time 'Do you want a scone?' 'No thanks' I would say. 'What's wrong with them? Am I not a good enough cook for you?' I just could not win…. [Steve]

The display of strategies to evade or reduce his stepmother's wrath, although unsuccessful on this and many other occasions, can be seen as an early sign of Steve's understanding of the nature of his suffering and a previously hidden ability to take aversive action. Deliberately choosing a 'fairly small' scone, or politely saying 'No thanks' is evidence of Steve's development of resourceful techniques to control 'the dynamics of disorder and by the exploration and development of hitherto unseen personal capacities' (Riemann and Schütze: 121). There is evidence too in Jane's narration of early techniques of 'good' behaviour as she endeavours to regulate the forces of disarray in her life:

I felt like I was always trying to make my mum better…um…you know if I was a really good girl my mum would be nicer toward me and she wouldn't be angry, or sad…and um…or cross…. [Jane]

Not only was Jane's 'good girl' action scheme an attempt by her to avoid the consequences of her mother's negative moods, it was perhaps additionally, what Prins (1995) points to as a sign of emotional neglect, a means whereby the child in the absence of a positive significant other attempts to 'turn their parents or caretakers into such persons' (1995:66). Mirroring the behaviour she wished to receive from her mother was unsuccessful for Jane. The futile attempts to make 'mum better' were internalised by her as personal failure, which served to reinforce negative expectations in her everyday affairs and further damage her fragile identity.

Ella, as discussed earlier, was sexually abused by her father from the age of three. The abuse was carried out frequently until Ella was sixteen years of age and her father died. An early coping strategy developed by Ella throughout this period in her life was dissociation: 'Dissociative symptoms exist along a continuum, ranging from common experiences such as daydreaming and lapses in attention, through déjà vu phenomena, to a pathological failure to integrate thoughts, feelings, and actions' (Atchison and McFarlane, 1994). Examples of these extremes could range from driving home from work on 'automatic pilot' and failing to remember the journey, to taking 'mental blackouts' during habitual sexual abuse and not being able to remember some or all of the experience. The psychiatric term 'dissociation' is highly associated with children who have been sexually abused and more so when the abuse began in early childhood and continued over a long period (Chu et al., 1999). Periods of dissociation are commonly reported by individuals who self-injure, a theme repeated in this study. The term refers to a failure to mentally integrate overpowering thoughts, emotions, awareness and/or memories (that would normally be processed together), because they are too traumatic for the conscious mind. Instead they are separated from each other, compartmentalised and often rendered inaccessible to one's consciousness or voluntary recall (Steinberg, 1994). For example, a sexually abused child may repress all, or certain, memories of abuse (i.e. the act itself, what was said by the perpetrator) or remember only some of the details (i.e. smells, pain, details of furniture, or décor). This process is also known as 'splitting', a term first coined by French psychiatrist Pierre Janet to describe a defence mechanism used against the psychological effects of inescapable and overwhelming traumatic experiences (Van der Kolk and Van der Hart, 1989). Dissociative periods may occur not only during actual traumatic episodes but also in later life as a way to deal with stress as well as intrusive memories of past abuse. Ella suffered from such flashbacks which can be triggered in a number of ways, often by the innocent actions of others. She recalled an incident when her brother playfully surprised her from behind while she was standing at the kitchen sink:

> I would take flashbacks... I can't even stand at the sink cos he [her father] would come at me from behind... When I was about 21, I was washing up a few dishes for her [mother] and my brother came up behind me. I lifted a hammer that was sitting on the draining board and went nuts. I didn't hit him or anything but I told him never to come up behind me like that. I could see in my mother's eyes that she knew why. [Ella]

The leaking of memories into consciousness can also be prompted by the sight of certain objects or smells. Ella was reminded of her father in everyday life:

> I could be standing in the shop and see Park Drive cigarettes behind the counter... the ones my Da smoked... and that's enough to set me off. [Ella]

In common with others abused over a long period, Jane developed the ability to 'remove' herself on demand when psychological thoughts became overwhelming. However in later life she also dissociated without any apparent conscious effort. She describes such episodes of dissociation:

> I would be sitting calmly and then my Da would come into my head. And its weird cos he never speaks to me in it. Its really freaky and I think I'm going mental... Or I would be peeling potatoes or something and I kind of blank out... People say 'I was at your door'. Or, 'I was calling you'. And I don't hear anything... I don't even hear the phone ringing or anything... Its like I'm in the year 2006 and suddenly I'm back in 1970... And I can see everything so clearly. I can see everything the way it was in that house... It's nearly like watching a video.... [Ella]

This unique method of adaptation to suffering can be viewed as a desperate action scheme of escape which allows individuals to psychologically 'survive' unbearable situations in which they find themselves. This ability to remove oneself emotionally from an experience can become a regular occurrence. Although highly adaptive in relation to coping with extreme psychological cost, this strategy is detrimental in other areas of the individual's life. For example, it can be difficult to control aspects of dissociative periods such as determining when they begin or end. In addition, such periods of dissociation tend to leave the individual feeling disconnected from 'reality', which they often describe as a 'dead' or 'unreal' feeling. Self-injury is reported here and elsewhere as an act which serves to bring dissociative episodes to an end.

Maltreatment and developing identity

Does your Da do this?

A combination of lack of understanding and confusion, due in large measure to immaturity (which exposed them as vulnerable targets of abuse in the beginning), meant that the full scale of what was happening was not fully registered at the time of the original maltreatment. At young ages, society's repulsion or taboos surrounding what these adults do to them is often beyond comprehension. Feelings of anxiety, uncertainty and general suffering pervade routinely. As children develop, however, so does their capacity for increased understanding of themselves and their position in relation to the world. For many study participants who suffered in this way, a certain point in the trajectory was reached in which what had passed as 'normal' up to that point could no longer be viewed as such. The development of the 'generalised other' (Mead, 1934), whereby children took on the attitude of the wider community, opened up a different and horrific perspective of their suffering than had been available to them previously. For example, sexual relations with your father is not 'normal' in any society, but that is what had been happening to them. For some study participants, this period represented the core of the trajectory due to the extreme effect such a realisation of their experience had on their identity. Tracey and Ella had both been sexually abused repeatedly by their fathers. For Tracey (a 39-year-old single and unemployed woman), the sudden shock event of watching a sex education video at school blasted the full horror of her victimhood into the centre of her already fragile identity. Others, like Ella however, were not quite certain in the beginning that the relationship with her father was not like those of other children. For her, the process of becoming aware that this was sexual abuse was gradual:

> …. When I was young I didn't question it. I hated it and must have known enough to say nothing about it. But I wasn't sure…I was going to ask someone in school you know 'Does your Da do this?' You know, thinking it was normal. But then I got to about twelve and I started thinking 'No that's not normal. You just don't do these things'. And then I just went into my ma and said 'Mammy, my Da's doing things to me and I'm not sure if its right or wrong'. I didn't know it was normal or abnormal until I was getting older…. You just accept it cus its your Da…. [Ella]

The realisation of the enormity of one's suffering can have a deep impact which penetrates the core of the individual's identity. Those who are affected in this way may feel shameful or 'strange' to themselves and alienated in relation to others, which forces a deeper conditioning of state of mind in which the mood of suffering predominates. They can no longer carry on as before and feel driven by powerful outer forces over which they have no control and only a limited degree of understanding. In attempting to regulate her overwhelming emotions, Ella overdosed on painkillers. She survived and soon afterwards she began to self-injure.

For Steve, a strategy to end physical and emotional abuse was to report maltreatment to social services. He recalled how at the age of 13 or 14 years he confided in a social worker. His report led to a court protection order being filed against his father and stepmother and his subsequent placement in a number of 'children's homes'. This is what Riemann and Schütze (118) term 'a deep biographical irony'. A new trajectory – one of sexual abuse, emerges out of the attempt to escape the emotional and physical abuse at home. Steve could have no idea that his action in attempting to end one type of abuse would, in fact, germinate another. He recalls this extremely painful memory:

> I was about 13 or 14…. At mealtimes a houseparent would sit at your table to take charge and give out food. You had to ask

'Could I have a piece of bread?', 'Could I have a cup of tea?' and they would pour it. I was always getting threatened with the bad boys home…. You know like Borstal? And then um…. One of the staff…Edward…took an interest in me…. And at nights he would come into my room…. And he was threatening me…. And then….[long tearful pause]…. He was abusing me. [Steve]

It was at this point that Steve's self-injury began. Similarly, for those who did not suffer sexual or physical abuse but lived in invalidating environments all the same, similar conditioning can be observed. The impact of Jane's childhood of repressed negative emotion, keeping 'everything inside' and being a target for school bullies, was forced to a head by the break up of her relationship with a manipulative boyfriend.

A central premise of the trajectory process according to Riemann and Schütze involves the effect that suffering a devastating pivotal experience (or series of experiences) has on one's emotional wellbeing. These authors use the phrase 'crossing the border from an intentional to a conditional state of mind' (127) to explain the ways in which the trajectory can totally confound the individual's psychological state and his or her relationship with the self and others. This phase of the trajectory can be seen to affect the person in a number of areas: He or she can be left feeling dominated by formidable external powers over which there is, at that time, little understanding or control.

[It has] the effect of falsifying the expectations of a normal course of affairs. The person realises that s/he is driven by powerful outer forces and that the use of familiar strategies for social and biographical action is not possible anymore. Disorientation with regard to the world and oneself becomes dominant, and the capacity for coordinated social action with a complex division of labour and (serial) articulation of activities is suddenly extremely weakened (at least under certain aspects and for a while). However, the capacity for managing the small necessities of everyday life is basically upheld. (Riemann and Schütze: 127)

It could be argued that the individuals in this study did not cross from the intentional state of mind to the conditional as many of them grew up in environments of invalidation and abuse in which the developing 'self' was already affected.

It is also interesting to note here the appearance of certain textual indicators of disorder which are evident when people remember and narrate unprepared biographical narratives. Such textual indicators can be even more evident when the narrator wants to include emotionally difficult and painful memories. These signs of disorder in the transcript can take a number of forms:

> ...e.g. the occurrence of several hesitation phenomena and of numerous unfinished sentences; paralinguistic signs of emotion; narrative self corrections and complex background constructions which means; interactive attempts to circumvent certain elements of the story line. (Riemann and Schütze: 124)

Steve wants to disclose that he was sexually abused, but seems to be having a difficult time relaying such a traumatic story and so adopts a somewhat involved backdrop to ease the telling of the sexual abuse narrative. He begins by recalling his age ('I was about 13 or 14'), when sexually abused by his houseparent, but then hesitates and changes to a background construction of highly controlled mealtimes before going back to the point of the story. The background construction is followed by further hesitation 'and then um...', then a vague euphemistic reference to his abuser having taken 'an interest' in him. The narration then leads to unfinished sentences, more hesitations, attempts to skirt around the main issue with 'At nights he would come into my room...And he was threatening me'. It takes another long tearful pause before Steve can finally and squarely release the painful information: 'He was abusing me'.

The disorder in how the traumatic event is stored in the memory can be seen in Ella's narrative of her recollection of the day she disclosed the abuse to her mother:

> I remember it really well. I even remember the date when I told her because it was May and it was the day of the May procession [Catholic feast day]. I told her and she said 'Get up and get him'. And I went up to the procession for him. The thing that sticks in my head...not what I said to him or the row after. I remember he was in the procession holding the statue of Our Lady and all

I could think of was 'How dare you hold that?'...He looked like a child who'd been caught stealing sweets when I told him what my ma wanted him for...I remember what he was wearing. He was wearing a blue shirt with a small collar. He was always spick and span...and I remember the net curtains hanging in the doorway and him standing there with that look on his face, like a child who had been caught out being bold. [Ella]

Although Ella alludes to having a strong recollection of the event, we can clearly see the fragmentation in her ability to store and recall certain details of the painful experience. Such 'splitting' of the experience in her mind is evident as she hyper-focuses on certain detailed elements of the memory, such as those pertaining to the religious statue, what her father was wearing, the look on his face and the curtains behind him. Her memory appears sketchy in relation to other parts however, that is, she cannot recall the particulars of what she said to her father or her parents' verbal exchange.

Sliding deeper

I thought I was going crazy

Steve's whole childhood up until this point had been disfigured by endless emotional and physical abuse. His sense of self had been damaged by years of maltreatment by the significant others in his life – both parents, stepmother and matron. Now sexual abuse at the hands of his houseparent added a new and horrendous dimension to his long trajectory of suffering. He pushed Edward to the floor and ran away from the children's home. He was caught and returned however and his humiliation continued when he was forced to apologise to Edward in front of his social worker and a psychiatrist. Steve did not report the abuse because he assumed that no one would believe him. Previous strategies employed to end or reduce his suffering by relying on others had either failed or had indeed worsened his situation. Steve at this point was left feeling what Riemann and Schütze (122) term, 'severe disorientation' and 'disconnection from the world':

I was so confused at this point. I couldn't think straight at all. I mean how much shit can one person take? The people who are supposed to be protecting you are just as bad as the rest of the bastards. I was only a kid. I was confused. I felt like there was no rules, no order, no protection, nothing could be relied on. I mean I can sort of put it into words now at the age of 40. But back then it was just like staring into mud. A child's mind can't even begin to process that shit. [Steve]

Similarly, as Ella's trajectory took hold and increased in strength, further elements were drawn into the mix and she slid deeper into suffering. Ella's abusive father was a highly respected member of the community who worked on a voluntary basis for his local church. His friendship with the local clergy reinforced the confusing messages being received by Ella:

He [her father] was always having the priests round for dinner and stuff. He was always doing voluntary work for them. They thought he was the salt of the earth...and then he would come home and rape me. [Ella]

A father who subjects his daughter to severe and prolonged sexual abuse is regarded by society as deplorable, yet Ella's was held in high regard by that same society. She made the abuse known to her mother which, according to Ella, earned her father 'a bit of a telling off'. The abuse was allowed to continue. Both Steve and Ella's abusers were held in high esteem by others, which served to increase the psychological control they had over their young victims. Jane's attempts to 'make her mother better' failed. She was also a target for a school bully. Her relationship with an emotionally abusive boyfriend had a further detrimental effect on her self-image, as did the subsequent breakup. In all three cases we can observe the trajectory, much like a snowball rolling down a snow-covered mountain, building up speed, gaining in size, swallowing up everything in its path and increasing in force as it goes. The exhausting work required to maintain a degree of equilibrium in one's day-to-day existence and attempts at taking control (which can lead to more suffering) accumulates to further energise the trajectory's power, sending the sufferer into a 'downward spin' (Riemann and Schütze: 128).

Here, we can see the trajectory at its most powerful. It culminates at this point after a series of events and is epitomised by extreme confusion as to the relationship with oneself and others. At this point all three participants discussed here reached a breakdown of self-orientation. Riemann and Schütze describe the consequences. Their observations are worth quoting at length as they encapsulate the essence of the trajectory dynamics on the self-injuring individual:

> For the time and moment being, the person experiences the total breakdown of her/his organisation of everyday activities…The world becomes totally strange; the focus of attention to the normal affairs and objects of everyday life is distorted; there is a massive, piercing or nagging pain of being separated from the existential world of normal life; for some time no other sensations and emotions are possible…Of course the devastating and paralysing experience 'that nothing is possible anymore' has implications. The person's orientational and emotional relationship to her or his identity is lost, at least for the time of the peak crisis: the person feels totally strange to her or himself, knows that she/he cannot trust her/his capacities anymore, and does not understand her/his own strange reactions to the unexpected events. (Riemann and Schütze: 129)

Ella described reaching this point: 'I couldn't stick it no more…him doing that to me'. She took an overdose of painkillers with the intention of killing herself at the age of eleven. She describes the incident with her mother and sister. Her sister was also being abused by their father. No medical assistance was sought:

> My ma and my sister, who had also been abused, walked me around the living room floor after they found me lying on the bathroom floor…They didn't do nothing. All they did was walk me around the sitting room and my sister said 'He's touching her too'. And nothing was done. [Ella]

For many in similar circumstances, this breakdown of self-orientation marks the beginning of another attempt to take control in the form of self-injury.

Self-injury as escape

A tiny little cut…it made me feel instantly better

A basic desire to survive his terrible situation led Steve to self-injure (at this stage without much control) with a razor blade. He found the act beneficial both emotionally and physically. It facilitated a means of temporarily reducing extreme psychological distress and of escaping his abuser:

> ...And then I got a hold of some razor blades and um started slicing my wrists. And then I noticed this was getting me some time in the hospital. It wasn't attention seeking, but when I was in there he [Edward] couldn't get any access to me cus I was on 24 hour watch. But then after that and I had to go back I started self-harming again. [Steve]

Like Steve, most participants in this study recounted that their self-injury began spontaneously, in response to unbearable psychological turmoil. In fact, many indicated a belief that they had 'invented' self-injury. Some however, reported that they had already heard of self-injury from friends or on television. Jane, for example 'Got the idea off TV' and in the immediate aftermath of breaking up with an emotionally abusive boyfriend, she:

> ...went upstairs to the bathroom and found a pair of scissors up there and cut my left wrist...A very, very, tiny little cut...but um...that was the first time and it made me feel instantly better. [Jane]

This finding supports recent sociological studies on self-injury that have pointed to an upsurge in self-injury as being a behaviour which, increasingly, is being learned from sources other than the self. Media attention, internet sites and a number of celebrities have drawn attention to the phenomenon since the mid-1990s (Adler and Adler, 2007, 2011; Hodgson, 2004). Whether self-learned or other-learned however, the functions of the behaviour for all participants remained similar: It is a way to regain psychological integrity.

Ella's first episode of self-injury also came at a crisis point. She had discovered her mother's dead body. After a short period, her brother also died and she was awarded guardianship of his three children, all of whom suffered from a chronic illness and required substantial amounts of daily care. She had previously taken an overdose and had relied heavily on alcohol and drugs since her teen years. At one point she resorted to 'wrecking the house' in an attempt to vent unwanted emotions but reported that having to clear up afterwards dissuaded her from repeating the act. Self-injury was an option which according to Ella, 'didn't hurt anyone else'. She was aware of the negative affect these other actions would have on the children living in her house. Self-injury seemed the logical option as it was an escape which was detrimental to no one else.

The main function of the action scheme of self-injury for Steve, Ella and Jane was, from its initiation, the instant release of unbearable psychological stress:

> I felt like my head was going to explode...Like I wanted all the stuff out of me. [After cutting] I felt better...It was like...The only way I describe it...when you do it you feel such a relief. It's better than smoking, better than sex, better than anything. You feel calm and in control. [Ella]

> It feels brilliant...Absolute pure relief and calm...the pain goes away and everything becomes more focused...Pain release...Getting rid of the pain in your head when you just can't deal with it anymore...It puts you into a twilight zone...You know cutting and then watching the blood and patching up. [Steve]

> I kept everything inside me and it came out through my cutting. And when I was 17 even though it was triggered by the boyfriend, I found that it was a great...relief, because it was the only way I could get out what was inside me...I can't talk to anyone but I can get it out this way...the release of pressure that I got...Um...I didn't know how to release it any other way...At that time I was very depressed and suicidal. The cutting helped me feel less suicidal...I often reached the point when I felt suicide was my only option and cutting helped me go a little bit further. It was a survival tactic...It sort of lessened the pressure for me and it was my way of surviving. [Jane]

Most individuals after giving the reasons and benefits of self-injuring also revealed a sense of guilt and shame at having cut themselves and having to deal with new problems such as covering up scars, and having to deal with the reactions of others. Self-injury however usually begins in times of crisis, with most individuals feeling like they have no choice in the matter. Many view it as the lesser of two evils (the other being more serious self-harm or suicide). The immediate benefits of cutting oneself in a period of deep psychological turmoil can outweigh any social or personal costs that may be incurred, costs however that have to be faced at some point.

One might ask why self-injury? One possible explanation as to why individuals begin to self-injure perhaps has something to do with a lack of alternative. Most people who self-injure begin in early adolescence when accessibility to other means of relieving psychological pain is usually restricted. Other maladaptive alternatives such as those found in alcohol and drugs abuse are often difficult to acquire (although, as discussed in Chapter 7, many of the people who spoke to me went on to alternate between self-injury and other self-harming behaviours).

The theoretical concept of trajectory (Riemann and Schütze), as presented here, offers a new approach to the understanding of the process of suffering for people who self-injure. Various stages in the process can be identified. These are not meant to be viewed as a rigid progression which runs mechanically and inflexibly. Similarly, it is not assumed that all people who have experienced a trajectory of suffering will self-injure, or conversely, that all self-injuring people have suffered in this way. Rather it provides an understanding of the main features in the process of suffering, allowing for varying degrees of agency and action on the part of the individual and an insight into the role and purpose of self-injury. Many people who self-injure have suffered from negative experiences, usually (but not always) in childhood. It could be argued that they were born into a trajectory of suffering which wreaks damaging consequences on the developing self. In the early stages of the process individuals may have little understanding of the source of their suffering and their ability to take charge of their life's circumstances may be tightly restricted. There is manipulation and control from outside sources. Self-injury under these conditions can begin (whether the individual has learned about it from the self or from another source) as a desperate action scheme of escape. Even during periods which are not characterised by distressing experiences, people can feel the effects of the 'trajectory' in their relationships with self and others.

Chapter 6 deals with stigma as well as other social and personal costs incurred by people who self-injure.

Once established in this way, self-injury and its meanings for those who use it can continue to evolve and develop in conjunction with the individual's relationship with, and understanding of, the source of suffering and life circumstances in general. This stage in the trajectory is characterised by the establishment of opportunities to reflect on one's suffering. Exploration and increased understanding of one's position can open the possibility to what Riemann and Schütze refer to as the person 'mobilising biographical work and creativity' (Riemann and Schütze: 121). One of the main features to stand out when one's knowledge is expanded in this way is the possibility to gain a greater degree of control to manage, even manipulate certain aspects of their self-injury. The ability to assert control in some aspects of the trajectory of which self-injury is part is discussed in the remaining chapters.

5
Self-injury Rituals

'This girl named Dawn' [by Dawn]

Do I feel there is a purpose in this?
Is this a ritual bloodletting to cleanse,
Or to remind
This is us stabbing in the mirror in the dark
We don't like what we see
Outside our houses and inside our sleeves
I am a veteran
I am one of the few
I feel this can get better
It could be made better
By us and by the societies
In which we exist
We are their subculture
We are held up and let fall

Think for a moment about self-injury. Now think of self-injury alongside the word 'ritual'.

The climax of the ceremony is the Gazing-at-the-Sun dance, which portrays the dangers of a warrior's life, namely, Capture, Torture, and Release. The dancers are 'captured' by warriors while women sing songs of grief…Incisions were made on their backs and chests and pieces of wood with attached leather thongs were inserted under the cut muscles. The thongs of some dancers were attached to buffalo skulls, but others had the thongs attached to the top of the Sacred Pole. They then danced; those who were attached to the pole were hoisted into the air while they gazed at the sun. They then struggled to break free of their bonds. Some unable to stand the pain, were cut free. Others successfully struggled until the wooden skewers ripped through their flesh; sometimes friends added their weight to the dancers and pulled hard until the flesh gave way. The pure in heart able to withstand this religious ordeal expected to receive a vision which, when understood, would make clear the meaning and course of their lives. (Favazza, 1996:12–13)

Is this colourful depiction of the Sun Dance of the Plains Indians in the United States an accurate depiction of many people's interpretation of 'ritual' involving a form of self-injury? If so it has perhaps been inspired by the popularisation of this representation in cinemas and on television, such as the film *A Man Called Horse* (1970). Within academic literature, ritual has tended to be associated with studies of religion. It looks, in particular, at how rites of passage which separate the sacred from the profane to mark changes in social life, identities and status (Durkheim, 1971). Rituals are also, importantly, ways to manage related tensions and anxieties. For example, a funeral is a ritual which is not restricted to marking the loss of a family member, friend or colleague. It also eases distress and angst, and affirms social ties among the living. It is a ritual for the living (Radcliffe-Brown, 1952). Similarly, a wedding not only formally celebrates the marriage of two people, but also eases apprehensions associated with changes in status and identities, and the coming together of two families.

Rituals are not confined to religious occasions of ceremony and formality, nor are they so far removed from everyday life. Ritual elements can be observed in both sacred and profane action. They can be seen in ordinary, everyday life, in what Goffman (1967) refers to as 'interaction rituals'. Rituals are a fundamental component, present in all areas of social life and are a vital way by which both groups and individuals manage problems and stresses encountered day-to-day (Goffman, 1967). A simple handshake between friends is viewed as a sign of their familiarity. Between people who are meeting for the first time it may also be a way to 'break the ice' by easing tension. In a business setting a handshake also symbolises the opening and closing of a meeting and the sealing of a deal between business associates.

What about solitary rituals? A bedtime routine could be seen as an example of a solitary ritual. It could be argued that turning off all electrical appliances and lights, closing doors, brushing teeth and washing one's face are all procedures done for practical reasons of safety and hygiene. However, could it also be possible that the process surrounding such a night-time routine, also plays a symbolic role in the way we contentedly settle down for the night? Does the bedtime routine also contain symbols of relaxation, a time for pondering the day's events and to contemplate tomorrow? Do acts which are initiated for one purpose take on additional symbolic meanings?

When it comes to aspects of behaviour, there is little which cannot be ritualised and self-injury is no exception. The term 'ritual' involves a range of complexities regarding definitions, meanings and functions that may vary according to time and culture and according to the particular orientation of the scholar (Grund, 1993). A detailed review of the literature on ritual in the social sciences is not within the remit of this book. However, in presenting a comprehensive picture of ritual in relation to self-injury, observations from comparative work in other areas (such as drug use) will be made when relevant. For this study of self-injury, the definition used by the anthropologist Carter is helpful:

> [Ritual]…must involve repetitive action, be kept in limited contexts, reflect basically uncritical acceptance of some value, quality, attitude, or belief, and in some way convey to the individuals hope that he will be helped in coping with his situation and in facing life with renewed vigour and confidence. (Carter, 1977:109)

In this chapter we will explore the meanings and functions of rituals in self-injury for people who practise it.

Rituals of self-injury

To make sure I didn't get any infection…It became part of the whole ritual of it

Ritual in self-injury is a new area of research. As presented in this study, it is a solitary ritual. It is also a private ritual except occasionally under extreme conditions when, for example, individuals are residing in institutions such as prisons or psychiatric settings. The solitary rituals of humans are extremely difficult to research. They have however been studied more intensely in animal societies where they have been observed as a reaction to extreme and confusing stimuli and other anxiety-inducing circumstances which exceed the animal's ability to manage sufficiently (Grund, 1993; Portman, 1961). Examples of these solitary animal rituals are pacing and rocking (Grund, 1993). They are used to reduce anxiety (Wallace, 1966). Similarly in solitary rituals of people who self-injure, it is when they are forced to endure trauma and anxiety from an uncontrollable outer force that they self-injure to 'channel and ameliorate the experienced stress and to prevent harmful responses' (Grund, 1993:7). For those who self-injure, ritualisation maximises the behaviour's ability to regulate negative emotions. The neutralisation of distress and anxiety is enhanced and additional factors relating to surroundings, apparatus and the actual process take on additional symbolic meaning and are drawn into the ritual itself.

Most participants in this study, when talking about how they began to self-injure, reported initial accidental discovery of the behaviour. Some had learned about it from other sources, such as the internet, media, magazines, television dramas and documentaries. Two individuals heard about the behaviour from a friend or someone at school. Dawn reported having found out about self-injury in popular magazines.

> I'd heard and read a bit about it, but I never really thought about it. It's just something that people do…in magazines…and I remember thinking 'That's just crazy stuff'. But I didn't know that it would ever happen to me, or that it happens so widely in Belfast, or anywhere. I thought it was something that happened in England, or something, and was in magazines. But whenever it happened to me, I fell into the whole trap without even realising what it was all about. [Dawn]

Jane had watched a television drama which featured self-injury and made a deliberate decision to try it herself:

I can't remember what the programme was but I remember think-ing 'I wonder if that would work for me?' So I'm guessing that it was some sort of release of anger and it worked. I tried it and it was instant … It was a rush, a really pleasant rush. It released anger and pressure. [Jane]

The majority of the people who spoke to me had not heard of self-injury before they began to use it themselves. Sam's introduction to cutting was at the age of twelve when he accidentally hurt himself with a broken glass.

I was picking up the glass and cut myself by accident. It made me feel better and then I started doing it on purpose. [Sam]

Susan had never heard of self-injury, however, neither was her first experience accidental. The frustration she felt while looking after two elderly and terminally ill parents became such a strain that while unpacking some medical equipment one afternoon while alone, she began to cut herself. She described what happened.

I was up the stairs and I was opening the boxes with a box-cutter and I was taking the stuff out and putting it into drawers … the tears were just trailing down my face … my mammy was … she was taking a nap in the afternoon and my daddy … he was always just sitting in the chair dozing off and I just looked at the box-cutter and I just started cutting … I felt stronger and I was able to cope a lot more for a few weeks until I felt that way again and I thought 'Well that made me feel better before, so I'll do it again'. So the next time it was more planned. It made me feel like I could cope again. I used the box-cutter again and the third time I used a Stanley knife. [Susan]

Using self-injury for the first time can often be impulsive and charac-terised by a lack of control, whether or not the initial experience was reported as being a deliberate or self-determined choice. Continuance of the behaviour may be reinforced by the many positive functions self-injury provides. In speaking to the people who took part in this book, it became apparent that most rituals involving self-injury do not become established until some time has passed and they are able to exert some control over the behaviour. These rituals focus on ways to maximise the self-injuring experience.

Tina reported that her first episode of self-injury was desperate and to a certain extent, uncontrolled:

> I remember the first time alright. I had a row with my mum…I just felt so angry and frustrated…I got a knife from the kitchen…I stabbed myself in the leg. I'm not sure what made me do it. It was impulsive. [Tina]

Nora used her position as a laboratory technician to obtain her self-injury implement:

> I started punching and hitting myself, but it didn't have the effect I was looking for. I couldn't relax. I worked in a lab at the time and one day I took some blades. I wasn't sure in my head what I was going to do with them at the time. The first place I cut was on my arms and that was quite a random thing the first time I did it. I felt release from it…after that I started to think a bit more about it…and the next time it happened it was much more methodical. [Nora]

When self-injury is used to deal with emotional distress, the act can become habitual. It is often not a long period of time after the initial episode of self-injury (which may have been, but not always, characterised by clumsiness and lack of planning) that the ritualisation of the behaviour takes hold. More control can be asserted in the act, and factors relating to where, when and how it is carried out, become important symbolic elements of the self-injury ritual, often becoming ends in themselves.

The surroundings

In order for self-injury rituals to function at maximum levels for the individual, the surroundings in which they take place must be prepared, both in terms of the physical and emotional environment. Self-injury is a 'loner' activity (Adler and Adler, 2005:345). Therefore the surroundings in which self-injury rituals take place are influenced first and foremost by the requirement of privacy. The majority of people who self-injure do so at home and in this study, participants living with other people were likely to use their bedrooms or bathrooms. The preferred time of day for the majority was usually in the evening. It was typically carried out when the person was alone and relatively sure that he/she would not be disturbed. Nora explains her preference for private surroundings:

THERESA: Did it mean more to you when you could take your time in the privacy of your bedroom?

NORA: Yea I felt like I got more out of it. Whenever I did it hurriedly in work there was more of an initial rush but it didn't last very long. When I did it at home I was able to think about it more and take my time. I just felt more relaxed and in control and it lasted longer. [Nora]

Private surroundings are not only required to deal with the practicalities of carrying out the ritual. Some participants pointed out that being alone allowed them to focus on their emotions in preparation for the act of self-injury, whereas when they were in the company of others, they were perhaps not able to concentrate on upsetting thoughts. Rachel illustrates this point:

[It was] always in the kitchen at home...I think there was a build-up to it. I knew I could only do it when my mum was out. So I had to wait until she went out. I think I only let myself get upset when I was alone because I knew I could do it...So maybe subconsciously I was planning it. [Rachel]

The negative feelings of loneliness, alienation, self-loathing, guilt and the like have been well documented in literature written from the point of view of people who self-injure. Such emotions can act as precipitating factors in the act of self-injury. In turn these distressing states are alleviated by the act (e.g. Harris, 2000; Miller, 1994). Rachel's comments illustrate her insight into her self-injury and raise two additional issues. First, self-injury involves negative emotions as a prerequisite. When the behaviour becomes highly ritualised, it may follow that self-injury is not only carried out in response to unbearable psychological distress. Psychological distress is a necessary precipitating requirement of the rituals and may be prompted by the individual in order to carry out the ritual. Second, if the requirements of a private space in which to perform the act of self-injury and to induce the required psychological state are not immediately available, people who self-injure can put off the ritual until a satisfactory space can be arranged.

For those whose self-injury became highly ritualised, it was noted that they became able to optimise the benefits of the behaviour. The more functionally rewarding rituals were those which involved the most significant amounts of control and planning. The more command individuals exercised in the rituals, the more rewarding they were reported to be. Study participants who lived alone had the most elaborate rituals, probably due to fewer restrictions regarding privacy, time and space. John, for example, recalled during the interview that his self-injuring in general was 'at its height' during periods of his life when he was living alone. He commented: 'It's an easier thing to do when you're on your own because you're not involving anyone else'.

The apparatus

Many people began to self-injure by using whatever method happened to be available to them at the time of the first deliberate or accidental act. They then progressed to using a specific implement to cut or burn. Tom was a 23-year-old university student whose uncle had been convicted of murdering his cousin and grandmother. His self-injury began at the age of 12 years in response to the emotional impact of the traumatic event. He recalls how he began to self-injure by hitting walls:

> The feeling was pure anger. I started punching walls…The physical pain took away from the trauma. It was all the emotion that I couldn't deal with. [Tom]

Tom progressed from striking hard surfaces to cutting himself with blades as part of his self-injuring rituals. He stated that during this time he missed his murdered family members and was feeling isolated and helpless while living away from home at university. He found that cutting himself was not only easier to control than hitting walls, but it also helped him to take some control in his life in general. Self-injury involving cutting and burning is more likely to be ritualised than that involving hitting or punching. The participants of this study who hit themselves usually did it as an expression of rage, using fists, or throwing themselves against hard surfaces. Hitting seems to involve spontaneity and reduced control. By comparison, rituals involving cutting are characterised by the element of control and the command of a sharp implement. Cutting often involves less spontaneity and more planning and is therefore more often the focus of the self-injury ritual. Mike used both hitting and cutting. He was clear in his distinction between the meanings of the two methods:

> It [cutting] was very controlled…not hacking at myself at all. It was very controlled…There were times when I went and got a knife and sat down with it…Sometimes I would buy a razor blade to do it. The time when I was hitting and punching myself wasn't as controlled as when I cut myself…With me it was more of a flare-up…it [hitting and punching] wasn't often planned…It would be an outburst of rage against myself. [Mike]

Blade fixation

Recent research with drug users has looked at the complex relationship between the individual and the needle as part of the drug-using experience (McBride et al., 2001; Pates, 2001). Similarly this study has made comparable observations on the significance of the blade, an aspect of self-injury research that has also, thus far, been neglected. While some of the participants did not mention a cutting implement as having any important significance, others disclosed a secretive and 'special' relationship with blades. For example, in one of her poems, Dawn (age 21) alludes to her blade as a treasured possession, on opening a drawer where she keeps it to discover a spider crawling around:

Spiders [Poem by Dawn]

> Spiders lift themselves over my favourite blade
> And crawl, dragging their limbs
> Over my things

The condition of the blades was often reported as important. Many participants expressed a need for 'sterile' or 'new' blades every time they self-injured. The lack of pain during self-injury is another theme which has been noted in earlier research (Adler and Adler,

2004; Favazza, 1996). Some people in this study, however, described feeling the sensation of pain towards the end of the episode, signalling for them to end the ritual:

> I don't know why, but I don't feel any pain when I'm cutting my arm. I become so engrossed in it ... After I've made a few cuts, I might stop for a while and watch the blood ooze out ... Then I might start again. When I start to feel pain I know it's time to stop. [Tina]

For others, lack of pain lasted until after 'patching up', or even into the next day:

> I don't really feel pain during self-injury ... I don't really be aware of pain anyway ... not while I'm doing it. Even hours afterwards or even the next day, there's no pain. It does start to hurt eventually though. [Aoife]

Other equipment

Some study participants, when asked about the equipment they used to self-injure, reported that a knife or blade was the only apparatus employed, especially during self-injuring episodes which occurred before the ritual had fully developed. On further questioning it became clear that many of these individuals also incorporated additional equipment such as antiseptic, gauze, bandages and/or kitchen paper. Many of these items were incorporated initially for practical purposes such as those relating to hygiene and first aid. As the ritual developed, however, their inclusion became more than just practical necessities. They were drawn into, and became part of, the ritual itself. Nora and Molly, for example, both used antiseptic to aid with cleaning cuts and preventing infection:

> As I progressed with the planning of it I would have taken more care of it. With antiseptic wipes and Savlon [antiseptic brand name] to make sure I didn't get any infection with it and that became part of the whole ritual of it. [Nora]

Both women derived additional benefits from the inclusion of antiseptic in the ritual. The distinct aroma was recalled by Molly as enhancing the experience further:

After you cut yourself…the patching up is important to me too. I like the smell of the Savlon. It makes me feel clean or something. I feel better when I use it. It wouldn't be the same if I just covered it up and didn't use the Savlon. [Molly]

In addition to pieces of equipment, which were initially employed for practical reasons such as cleaning wounds or soaking up blood, other items were chosen deliberately for the purpose of experience maximisation. For example, music that matched the mood of the individual or the mood that s/he wanted to create was sometimes included. This became an important feature of Lena's ritual. The anger in the song chosen not only matched how she was feeling, it was also a symbolic representation of childhood. She revealed that the addition of music in her self-injury episodes was also a way to deliberately evoke childhood memories:

LENA: I would go to my room with a knife and put on 'Under the bridge' by 'The red hot chili peppers' on the CD player.

THERESA: Was it always that particular song? 'Under the bridge'?

LENA: Nods]

THERESA: Why that one?

LENA: Because 'Under the bridge' is like…an angry song. And whenever I was cutting myself I felt angry. And also whenever I was growing up…Me and my mates used to hang around under the bridge at Newtown. When I was feeling bad, I would put this music on to bring my emotions on even more and then I would be able to cut myself. [Lena]

For others, the inclusion of soft lighting, including candles, was a way of enhancing the ritual experience. Whatever was required for the ritual to take place, both in terms of surroundings and of apparatus, was of such importance in the ritual that participants waited until everything was in place. Aoife, for example, would postpone her self-injury if her partner and children were at home:

No matter how bad I was feeling, I would wait until Conor [partner] could take the kids to the cinema or swimming or something and I was sure I would have a few hours to myself. I mean I know I could just nip into the bathroom or something and use a blade then and there … And I suppose I have done that in the past … But I prefer to wait until I can do it properly, and then it's so much better. [Aoife]

The process

The actual process of the ritual can be viewed as a repetitive, self-perpetuating cycle which has varying emotional levels for the individual. The stages can be charted from the initial idea or notion to self-injure, through the actual act, to patching oneself up, and includes a period of anti-climax. The need to follow a familiar procedure is similar to that of needle fixated drug-users in the study carried out by McBride et al. (2001). In their research, respondents reported the 'central importance' of 'ceremony and following the right procedure' (McBride et al., 2001:1052). McBride and his co-authors also highlight the significance of the build-up to drug injecting. In fact, some of their respondents reported the build up as being of greater significance than the actual drug use itself.

Build-up

Hours, often days before a self-injury ritual takes place, individuals may feel the urge to self-injure and may begin the process of preparation. The beginning of this process can be marked as the moment when the urge arises or the decision is taken to self-injure. This decision may or may not be taken consciously. Some participants described beginning preparations without making a conscious decision to do so. Others were more definite in their decision. For example, Sally described how she knew on a Monday that on Thursday she would self-injure. The decision to self-injure is part of the ritual in itself. It leads to an increase in feelings of control from the moment the decision is taken and preparations begin.

Rewards were identified by study participants in each act of preparation. Steve referred to this part of the ritual as his 'calm, angry stage'. Some participants made attempts to avoid the ritual. For example, Anne's preparation for self-injury was the making of her cutting implement from a safety razor. She took time to disassemble a safety razor in the hope that the urge to cut herself would wear off by the time it was ready for use. In fact, the opposite happened.

During the time it took to prepare her cutting implement, the urge to cut herself usually intensified. The process became part of the ceremony, a period of emotional stimulation and build-up in which she psychologically primed herself for the climax of the ritual:

> Yes it was planned, because every time I cut myself, it takes a lot... It has to be sort of thought of because you make the thing you cut with. I made it with the normal razor that you would use for your legs, but obviously it's really hard to try and... You have to undo it, chop it up, prepare it and um... I was really glad that it took all that effort, because sometimes if you weren't really feeling all that bad, the whole thought that you had to go and prepare this razor just put you off. But other times... Usually... You just didn't care. You made it. You used it and that was it... You just wanted it to be ready. You just wanted to be able to cut. [Anne]

The acts of assembling apparatus and preparing surroundings are often done in a particular order, adding to the build-up of emotions. Steve describes this part of his self-injury ritual:

STEVE: There was a real structure to it. It's always in the evening. It's always with razor blades and the notion would come on me about two or three days before it. And then I would prepare my self-harm equipment. I would start thinking about it and then I would try to distract myself. But the thoughts actually become really intense because I'm really emotional you know... It's hard to describe... Really agitated. And then I would start preparing for it. I'd have loads of Kitchen roll [absorbent material], new blades every time... I'd be really clinical and clean about it. Sometimes I'd go as far as having sutures ready. I'd go and buy some of them. I'd buy bandages... Um... antiseptic liquid... And I'd be just sitting there in the living room with everything prepared... And I'd start thinking...

THERESA: What would you be thinking about?

STEVE: Usually about the stuff from the past. And what's going on, what's agitating me... It would be a combination of both the past, and stuff that's stressing me out in the present … And I go into a sort of trance … well maybe not a trance, more a composed state on the surface anyway, but with anger bubbling up underneath if you know what I mean. [Steve]

Climax

Once emotions have been allowed, or encouraged, to build to unbearable levels, the process moves to the climax of the ritual. It is often the most intensely controlled part of the ritual, with some participants revealing in the most private and detailed accounts precise control over minute details of the cutting. Steve gave a particularly intense account of the procedure:

STEVE: Usually when I cut I will count the seconds. How long it will be and how deep it will be … Its very controlled cutting … I mean I know when the razor blade goes in how deep I want it to go and how long it will be. I will count the seconds until I want it to stop …

THERESA: How many seconds?

STEVE: Forty seconds … This would be the length of time it takes to put the blade in, put pressure on it and draw it very slowly so you would get a good deep cut … I tried slashing but slashing doesn't last … It's over too quickly you know? … It would be two or three, or sometimes five cuts. [Steve]

How cuts are delivered can be controlled not only by counting the length of time the blade is used to administer each one, but also by maintaining uniformity. Nora describes this aspect as being a precise operation:

It was always very delicate. I always took great care when I was doing it. Each cut had to be the same. They all had to be the one length and in nice straight rows too. [Nora]

Other participants also counted the actual amount of cuts themselves in order to perform exactly the required amount. For example, Rachel counted 'twenty lines down each arm'. Eve not only counted her cuts, she also arranged them into a visually artistic pattern:

It's quite ritualistic actually…I reach the decision to cut and once that's done I sharpen the knife and get the alcohol wipes. I would start off quite measured and controlled and start cutting my left arm first. I can't stop with one arm. It has to be matching…so I move to the other arm then. When I say matching, I mean that from an aesthetic point of view. It has to look nice. I would do one arm in one direction first and then match up the other arm. Then I would go back to the first arm and change direction. There would be definite criss-crosses. [Eve]

Similarly, Dawn's ritual was characterised by pattern – in both preparation and in how she went about actually cutting her skin:

I'd just like, sit in the same position and just do the same pattern. I'd go upstairs and sit on my bed. And I had a wee box that I kept the razors with the blades in. And I'd just get the blade out and I'd sit and trail over in the same way each time. And it was always very small. Um…just like tiny…not even a centimetre long and not very deep. After that it became more than little nicks. They were always in a concentrated area…So say it was like, part of my elbow, they would always be really small, but there would be like 15 of them all in the same place, like within a wee tiny area. So it was like, I had a wee square and I had to fill it in with marks. [Dawn]

Some participants went as far as to cut words into the skin. For example, Nora cut words which matched her mood and how she was feeling about herself at the time of a particular self-injuring ritual:

It took me a while to do it. I took my time and I was feeling like a stupid bitch so that's what I cut into my leg. [Nora]

Tracey also cut words into her skin:

I felt like I was floating away, like I wasn't part of the world. I felt dead so I cut the words 'I am dead' onto my stomach. [Tracey]

Blood fixation

None of the 25 participants expressed an aversion to blood while self-injuring. In fact, for many, blood, just like the blade, played a central and critical role in the ritual. John referred to the sight of blood in similar terminology to Eve, when talking about her cuts: 'I liked the look of the blood. It was aesthetically pleasing to look at the blood'. Blood, not surprisingly, is a highly symbolic and central element in most self-injury rituals: 'There has to be blood. When I see it I feel relief' [Eve]. The relationship with blood for most individuals is summed up in a quotation from Nora, who became particularly adept at controlling the appearance and the exact quantity of blood desired:

> Oh yea ... I liked the blood ... If there was no blood it didn't work. If you didn't cut too deeply you'd get little bubbles of blood coming up and I always really liked to see that. I always thought that looked quite nice. It was so slow and really nice ... Whereas when you cut deeper the blood was a lot faster. Again it was a control thing ... It was slow release ... Like oozing it out ... The cut would have become more open then as you rubbed along it and you would have seen the whole length of the cut rather than just little specks, or wee bubbles of it. I always liked little bubbles. Like the first rush. That's when it hit you, you know? The actual cutting itself you wouldn't have felt it and I didn't feel anything until I was about to see the blood ... And then it was just ... 'Aahh' ... 'Everything is going to be OK'. [Nora]

Many, like those in Sutton's (1999) research focusing on the accounts of people who self-injure, associated blood with suppressed emotions. For example, Jane, as a child, was not permitted to show negative emotions:

> Mum was the only one allowed to be angry. If I was angry or I cried I was told I was pathetic. So I had to hold it in until I cut ... and then the blood was my tears. [Jane]

Marie also experienced this association between blood and emotion. She described the release of 'anger and hate and frustration' as 'blood flows, stuff flows with it'. Similarly for Mike, bleeding symbolised the mind ridding itself of unbearable distress:

> To bleed was to have a result ... you want to bleed out the anguish in your mind. And when I think back blood always came into

it ... to get out the suffering and the torture and the anger and the agony and the awful feelings and how you hated yourself and how you were so damaged ... so when I think back ... once I saw the blood I felt better. [Mike]

Ella's narrative of her ritual also posits the arrival of blood as a central and essential element. Its appearance signals the end of the self-injury episode as far as actual cutting is concerned:

THERESA: You mention the importance of blood when you cut yourself. What does blood mean for you?

ELLA: Like all the stress is out of me. All the build-up is in my head and I would just go and get the razor ... As long as I get blood, that's enough for me ... It feels good and that's what I need. I can stop then. [Ella]

The sight of blood during self-injury can also be symbolic of purification of the body (Babiker and Arnold, 1997). Mike referred to seeing his own blood as 'expunging' from himself of extremely painful emotions which he described as 'all the torture and the agony'.

For many, blood symbolised the end of the climax and the cutting part of the ritual. As Dawn remarked; 'It just completed the wee routine that made me feel better'. Many participants stated that they viewed the ritual as unfinished until the appearance of blood. However, as further stages in the procedure of the ritual can be identified, it could also be argued that blood symbolised the end of the climatic stage, the highest point in the ritual. There are two additional stages following the peak of the ritual.

Draw-out

After the climax of cutting, satisfaction can be drawn out further. Many people described how they derived comfort and relaxation from actions of 'patching up' after self-injury. Supporting other research, this study shows that tending to wounds allows an opportunity for self-soothing which is especially valuable when original trauma was not soothed (Smith et al., 1998). Some also described feeling 'clean' when injuries were washed in antiseptic liquid and dressed in bandages.

Steve reported that the psychological 'release' derived from self-injury 'lasted right through until patching-up time'. However, often the ritual does not always end with caring for oneself physically and emotionally, but can be drawn out with further self-injurious acts:

> I would also pick at cuts when they start to heal over, until they start to bleed again. Rather than go for the blades again you'd start to pick at the cuts. I get satisfaction from that too. [Steve]

Picking at wounds (whether originally self or accidentally inflicted) which are in the process of healing is not an unusual form of self-injury and was one of the methods mentioned in the introductory chapters. For many people who told me about their self-injury rituals this was a secondary method used mainly as a means of prolonging the beneficial effects of the ritual:

> Once the cut is there, I would find myself in the next few days picking at the scabs whenever I felt a bit anxious or stressed. Sometimes I don't even realise I'm doing it. I just be sitting there and I go into a bit of a daze and the next thing I know I'm bleeding again. [Tina]

Anti-climax

At this point, one might assume that the ritual has concluded. There usually follows, however, an anti-climactic stage which serves to reinforce those negative emotions involved in the instigation of self-injury. Even though individuals self-injure for a variety of reasons, they also generally take on society's notion of 'normative' convention (Adler and Adler, 2004). Feeling ashamed at this point was commonly expressed by the majority of participants:

> Then comes the guilt, like you shouldn't have done that. You should have stopped yourself from doing it. I'd feel quite down then after the high. It's a really low feeling and I'd be very remorseful for quite a few days after it ... I'd be quite depressed ... I'd become isolated and not really go out of the house at all. [Steve]

Scarring left by self-injury was one of the costs that many did not consider at the time of injuring. Nora illustrates this point:

Unfortunately it left scars. I hadn't thought about the scars. It never entered my head. I just thought it would just be a cut where it would heal and go. I didn't think I'd be left with tracks all up and down my legs and arms…That just didn't figure into it. [Nora]

However, as Rachel commented, the need to self-injure often outweighs any feelings of guilt or consequences of permanent scarring:

You're really ashamed of doing it cus you know you really shouldn't be doing it. But you have to…to make yourself feel better. It's like there's no choice at all really cus you know its gona make you feel better. So even though you feel terribly guilty afterwards and even though you know you're damaging yourself and scarring yourself, you sort of bypass those reasons not to do it and do it anyway. You're positive it will get rid of the bad shit in your head, if only for a while. And that's what it boils down to in the end. [Rachel]

The 'downer' experienced at the end of the procedure is an unfortunate component of the ritual for the individual and is one which feeds back into negative feelings which gave rise to self-injury to begin with. However, the certainty of assistance in regulation of emotions and other benefits, even though temporary, promotes cyclical repetitiveness of the ritual. This categorisation of the self-injury ritual into themes relating to surroundings, apparatus and process is not meant as a static model. Rather it reflects central features which can be observed and is intended as a representation of the basic elements of ritualised self-injury.

The functions of the ritual

Well there you go…'That's a cut'…a message to myself

Rituals can serve a number of functions according to the various circumstances of their occurrence (Grund, 1993; Partridge, 1977). Additionally:

The function may differ for different actors in the same ritual. Ritual may have multiple meanings and, even further, these do not necessarily have to be in alignment with the intentions of the actors. (Grund, 1993:8)

The participants of this study reported a number of benefits which are similar to those in other qualitative self-injury research. Individuals may gain from one or more of the benefits and these accordingly may vary between and within individuals and from one self-injury episode to another. Functions are described as: relief from emotional distress, distraction, self-punishment, a way to end dissociative episodes, communication, control, self-comfort, a sleep aid and a technique of suicide prevention. People, in addition, may derive pleasure from the behaviour. Ritualisation of self-injury, whether it is limited to simply choosing a particular time of day, or, more elaborately, involves considerable preparation and forethought, maximises these functions for the individual. Rituals can take self-injury to a new level of meaning for those who practise it.

Relief from emotional distress

The most common function described by all 25 study participants was the reduction and release of unwanted emotions which had become overpowering. Tina describes her self-injury as the only way she was able to achieve respite from negative emotions which were causing her extreme psychological distress:

> I can't describe how bad it can get in my head at times. It's more under control now than it was, but especially back then … the feelings would just build and build until I felt like I was gona die if I didn't get rid of them. When I cut myself … the relief is almost instant, what it does for you. It's like bursting an abscess that is causing you unbearable pain. [Tina]

Steve's self-injury was also his way to relieve himself of feelings of anxiety and depression:

> How would I describe what it does for me? … Relief, absolute relief … Pain release … Getting rid of the pain in your head when you just can't deal with it for one single second more. [Steve]

Distraction/focus

For Steve, in addition to allowing him some relief from unbearable feelings, self-injury also helped him focus more clearly on his situation:

> All the pain goes away and everything becomes more focused. I can think a bit more clearly after I've done it. I become...not only more focused on the cut and patching myself up, I can also focus better on life without this fog in my head. [Steve]

The need to be able to distract themselves from unbearable emotions and thoughts was perceived by many of the study participants as another function of self-injury. Nora used her self-injury to divert herself from unwanted feelings:

> ...my head was full of all these thoughts and I couldn't stop them. So I didn't know actually what I was thinking. Whenever I cut myself then it was something to focus on. It was a real thing. Whenever I couldn't deal with all these thoughts in my head I had something to focus on...something to look at and it was a real thing...and that was what I was going to concentrate on. [Nora]

Lena's self-injury was a way to focus on physical pain in preference to, and as a distraction from, psychological pain:

> It was like...I would rather have a physical pain than the emotional pain. I could focus on the physical pain and it eased the emotional pain. The physical pain was nothing compared to the emotional pain if you understand...and when I cut myself, it eased the pain in my head. [Lena]

Self-punishment

Many people who suffer abuse can blame themselves and think themselves deserving of the harsh treatment or neglect they have received from others. They may have been led to believe by their abusers that they were responsible for, or deserving of, treatment they received from others. In this respect, self-injury can be a form of self-punishment (Miller, 1994). Self-punishment can manifest itself in the full range of self-injuring methods. However, hitting, punching or banging one's body off a hard surface were more often used as a way to direct anger inwardly. Mike differentiated between meanings he held for the self-injuring episodes of hitting and those of cutting. Hitting and punching himself with his fists allowed emotions of anger and rage to be directed both at himself as a form of deserved self-punishment and symbolically at his sexual abuse perpetrators:

> I was trying to cope with the trauma of being abused and every-thing...It would manifest itself in self-hatred, self-loathing and actually, literally beating yourself up...battering your arms and legs until they were black and blue...Mostly it would be an out-burst of rage against myself provoked by something that would come to me about the abuse and I would take it out on myself by punching myself very hard. It was always tied up with the abuse issues. [Mike]

Cutting himself with knives, however, was Mike's way to bring that pain out from inside his mind and place it on the outside:

> Cutting myself at times, was a way of expressing...trying to put out...an outward form of the interior agony. You were wounded and tormented in your mind, and you were trying to externalise it. Because when it was internal it was as if it was going to destroy you...eat you up. [Mike]

Ending dissociation

The technique of dissociation, developed as a means to remove oneself emotionally from painful experiences can affect some peo-ple who self-injure. One of the positive functions of self-injury for many participants was that of psychological escape from emotional anguish. This was described as a sort of welcomed numbing effect: 'It puts you into a twilight zone' [Steve]. Sometimes however, it can be difficult to end dissociative episodes and involuntary periods of dissociation can be ended by self-injury. Individuals who self-injure often describe periods of feeling 'numb' or removed from the world around them, and the ritual is a way to reconnect them with reality.

It provides the body with a sudden and immediate 'jolt' back to reality (Herman, 1992). Mike describes a similar experience:

> [Self-injury is a way to]…root you back in reality…cus you used to think that you were disappearing from reality…the way of bringing you back into reality was to beat yourself very badly to make you feel 'Oh, I'm back in the world now cus I have a sore arm'…there were times when I felt like I was disconnected from reality…like I was totally disembodied…spaced out…I was walking around and I couldn't feel the ground under me even…like I had been cut adrift. To inflict pain on yourself is like a way to bring you back into the world. The numbness felt like death…trying to pierce the numbness…The word trauma is the word in Greek to pierce or stab. [Mike]

Communication

Klonsky and Muehlenkamp (2007:1050) suggest that self-injury may be an attempt (intentionally or otherwise) to 'elicit reinforcing responses' from others. Although Steve's initial self-injury resulted in hospital admission, this was a secondary and unintended dividend of the act as it inadvertently gained him temporary protection from his abuser. Self-injury was expressed as a form of communication by some of this study's participants. However, whereas the above authors propose the act as a form of communication to stimulate reaction in other people, the majority of this study's participants used it as a way to communicate with themselves. Self-injury as self-communication has been documented in previous qualitative research findings with people who self-injure (Adler and Adler, 2004; Babiker and Arnold, 1997; Harris, 2000; Solomond and Farrand, 1996).

Mike's self-injury was also a way of communicating his own feelings with himself, feelings which he believed could not be shared with or understood by others. He expressed a need to externalise unbearable anguish by cutting his arms.

> I cut myself with a knife and they were…a visible manifestation of hurt…something that looked unpleasant…something that looked nasty…just to have something there to say 'Well there you go'…'That's a cut'…a message to myself…It was for nobody else

to see. In fact I wouldn't have allowed anyone else to see it. It was a way of telling myself I suppose, that I had been hurt really badly and here was a wound…a big gash on my arm to prove it. Other than that, the hurt has to remain in your head, doing more damage…you think sometimes you've imagined what happened so you have to put it out there to see with your eyes. [Mike]

Bruising and scarring, for many, was also a symbolic representation of both the physical and emotional suffering that they had endured in their lives, whether or not the sensation of pain was present during the actual injuring episodes. Tina's scars are symbolic of not only painful memories, but also the sense of pride she feels in being able to carry on with life successfully in the aftermath of traumatic experiences:

When I look at my scars, I do feel some regret and some shame at having done that on myself…But then…when I think about it, I also feel proud of what I have come through. I have survived all the stuff that happened and in some ways I'm a stronger person. My kids are loved and cared for and my self-injury does not affect them. So it's like…even though I usually didn't feel the pain when I was doing it…they're battle scars and they are saying to me 'You're a survivor'. [Tina]

As mentioned, Nora and Tracey both cut descriptive words which matched their thoughts and emotions into their skin:

I can look at the words for ages afterwards and even when they have healed, the scars are still there and I can still faintly see this message to myself. Cutting words into my skin helps me to focus on something. It's like it's something outside of your head is telling you that it knows your pain. Sounds a bit schizo I know. I mean I don't have a split personality or anything. But it helps being able to express, even if it's only with myself. [Tracey]

Control and self-comfort and sleep aid

One of the major functions of self-injury reported across all participants was that of control. Often individuals' lives were characterised by lack of control over their circumstances, sometimes in relation to abuse or neglect issues. Whatever the reasons were for each individual, self-injury was reported as a means to assert control over the psychological pain they were enduring and as a follow-on, in other areas of life. Cutting was the form of self-injury most associated with taking control and was also the most ritualised of all the methods used. Mike differentiated between levels of control associated with cutting as opposed to those involved when hitting himself. Similarly, Sally controlled internal psychological pain by inflicting external physical pain:

> It feels good to be in control of your pain. For me cutting was a way of taking care of the pain inside me. It was the only thing I had control over at that time. I was powerless to stop the things that were happening to me and I cut myself to feel like I was in some control of the pain. [Sally]

The distraction technique involving counting the number of cuts inflicted was Lena's 'way of taking control of psychological pain':

> When I am counting the cuts, I am in control of when I start and when I stop and to be honest, control is a big issue for me. I need that sense that I have a say in things…in how I feel and when I'm cutting, that's how I feel. [Lena]

Re-enacting traumatic events as mentioned in the literature review (Miller, 1994) is a way to try to understand and control memories, and sometimes elements of meaningful events are symbolically incorporated into the rituals. For example, Lena's use of a particular song was symbolic of a painful childhood. The song helped her express anger and was a meaningful reminder of people and places in her youth. In addition to re-creating painful experiences for the purposes of trying to understand and somehow control them, self-injury is also an opportunity for self-comfort (Miller, 1994). The tending to wounds caused by self-injury is characteristic of what Grund (1993:3) refers to as, 'instrumental' versus 'symbolic' ritual action. The acts of cleaning up blood, washing cuts, wrapping wounds in bandages and general first aid are practical requirements that must be performed mainly for purposes of hygiene and infection prevention. They are also a practical distraction from emotional distress, as reported by Sam: 'Cleaning myself up is a distraction…it also helps me control what's going on in my head'.

Mirroring a function provided by communal ritual for the social group is that of healing for the individual who self-injures. On a symbolic level, tending to one's physical wounds goes a little way in trying to make up for, or compensating oneself for, soothing that did not take place at the time of the initial trauma, as this moving depiction of Aoife's suffering illustrates:

> When I cut myself, I…for a while…it gets all the anger and shit out of me. But then it's like…I think of this little girl…lonely and frightened in her bedroom, hiding from the world…and I want to put my arms around her and protect her from evil bastards that would hurt her and abuse her. In my head I reach out to her and tell her that it's OK and I wipe her tears and comfort her and tend to her pain…Of course you know the little girl is me…and I had no one to help me. No one to make things right. I try to go back in time in my imaginary time machine and make her all OK. [Aoife]

Although people benefit from control and self-soothing functions of the ritual, it would be remiss to claim that they are deluding themselves into believing that by changing a distressing story in their imagination that it changes in reality. It seems, however, that the revisiting of painful experiences opens an opportunity to rewrite them insofar as making the desired outcome more acceptable:

> If I had a wish list, it would have at the top…the things that happened then, didn't happen. Sometimes I think back and think of how I would have handled things if I had been today's me and not that little girl. I know it maybe sounds silly…and I know those things really happened, but it makes me feel better to think of a happier scenario. [Aoife]

Unbearable emotional distress as well as the physical and emotional effort required to regain control, plan and execute the ritual can exhaust the individual. Because self-injury is often carried out in the evening time, it becomes for some participants an aid to induce sleep. Many, in this study, described the ritual of self-injury in the evening as bringing on a drowsy feeling, or, as John referred to it, 'a post euphoric slump', enabling them to wind down for sleep. Susan's anxiety at bedtime was relieved by burning:

> if I was going to bed at night and I could feel myself getting all panicky ... like panic attacks and I would burn myself and it would stop it ... I would just keep burning until I felt calm enough to go to sleep. I wouldn't be able to relax enough for sleep if I didn't hurt myself like this. [Susan]

For Anne, cutting herself in the evening time was not only a sleep aid but also a form of escapism:

> There were two things I really liked if that makes sense. A cut, cover it up and go to sleep ... And that's just ... you know ... cutting, let it go, sleeping. It was just like running away. [Anne]

Anti-suicide

The link between suicide and self-injury is often blurred. It is not unusual for many people to think about suicide at some time or other, whether they self-injure or not. People who self-injure may go on to kill themselves, but as far as self-injury as emotional regulation is concerned, it is not about dying. It is about living, attempting to reduce distressing emotions and cope with life with assertiveness and self-determination. Many participants insisted that if they did not have self-injury as an outlet they would have attempted or completed suicide:

> It's not about suicide. I thought about suicide, but not by self-injury. It would be railway tracks ... Something quick ... Um ... But it's the same issues that I think about. Self-harm is the opposite to that ... It's bringing you back from that. So it's a method of self-protection because you think it's so bad and you want to kill yourself ... It's you talking yourself down cus that's what it does. It was a kind of survival mechanism at the time ... There's no doubt about it. There was nothing else. It has repercussions in the long term. But it tides you over at the time. [John]

Like John, Tina was sure that self-injury for her was a much lesser evil than what she felt were her other options:

> I have lost count of the times where I have felt suicidal and con-templated killing myself. I had it all planned out in my head and everything. You know, how I would actually do it and stuff. If I hadn't had self-injury I would have been dead many years ago. It was the only option open to me then. It works…it works really well as a way to take control of your mental pain. So when it came to decisions about how I was gona get rid of the shit in my head, the choices were, one, get rid of them permanently by killing myself and having done with it. Or two, cut myself and ease it, for a while anyway. [Tina]

The difference between suicide and self-injury is further clarified by Steve in terms of methods used in both scenarios:

> THERESA: Do you think about suicide?
> STEVE: Yes, all the time. But that's where my self-harm comes in. It stops me from going that far. And when I think about killing myself, it's not about cutting myself with a blade. It's usually by taking an overdose or something. [Steve]

Sally's suicidal thoughts also involved overdosing as a method. Her quote makes clear, the differences between the two methods of self-harm:

> it was like 'I don't want to be here…I want to die'…I really wanted to die. But cutting myself eased that and it did stop me from doing something more. Several times I thought…I've been to chemist shops and bought tablets, painkillers and that and thought I would take an overdose and not wake up. Just end the whole thing once and for all by overdosing. But cutting myself stopped me from doing that…I don't know why, I can't explain it but it helps me carry on and keeps me from topping myself completely. [Susan]

When discussing thoughts of suicide in terms of methods, those of cutting and burning were not considered. Although these are the most common ways to self-injure, when suicide is the intention, it is planned by other means:

> Self-injury is definitely not about suicide, not for me anyway. When I cut myself, it's to relieve some of the pressure. When I punch walls, it's more about directing anger and rage. Don't get me wrong, I've also thought about suicide. But if I was gona kill myself it would be like that... I'd jump off a bridge or something else violent and quick... that would be it, if I really didn't ever wana wake up again. [Tom]

Other methods of suicide contemplated, aside from overdosing and jumping from a height, were hanging and crashing a car into a wall. The suicide prevention function of self-injury reported by this study's participants is supported in other self-injury literature from the perspective of the individual (Babiker and Arnold, 1997; Pembroke, 1994).

Pleasure

Self-injury can evolve from being impulsive in character especially in the early stages to become much more premeditated, control-led and ritualistic as time goes on. Some participants, Steve for example, developed the rituals to such a degree that certain components of the ritual eventually became part of the motivation for self-injuring. Satisfaction and gratification can be generated in rituals when emotions and thought processes are stimulated. Consequentially, the desire for pleasure can become a reason to instigate the ritual (Grund, 1993). Those participants in particular who had particularly highly developed rituals reported a pleasurable experience which is comparable with needle fetishes among drug users (McElrath, 2006). Some of the terms used by Steve and others to describe feelings of pleasure that became heightened in self-injury rituals were 'Brilliant', 'Pleasing' and 'Nice'. In fact the pursuit of relief from psychological turmoil was no longer the only driving force behind acts of self-injury. Pleasure derived from the self-injury ritual became an end in itself and a central motivator. Steve's anticipation of the appearance of blood enhanced and heightened his enjoyment of ritualised self-injury. This narrative of his experiences uses comparable terminology employed to describe the effects of illicit drug use:

> It's like a ... high. Like when you are cutting you'd be watching the blood coming from your body and it's like [tearful] ... unbeliev-able. It's such a buzz. There's nothing like it for making you feel better.... [Steve]

For Lisa, the pleasurable feeling she attained from her self-injury was comparable to her experiences of inhaling solvents as a teenager:

> I hated myself, but cutting gave me a high, like sniffing glue which I also used to do when I was younger. It's fucking great after you've been feeling like complete shit ... You feel all light and floaty.... [Lisa]

The unpacking of the self-injury ritual has uncovered a complex set of observations. Although usually a solitary business, it serves some of the same basic functions of communal rituals traditionally discussed by sociologists: the main one of these being assistance in coping with one's circumstances and optimising one's competence in carrying on with life. The meanings and functions of the self-injury ritual can be fluid. They can vary between individuals and can even change between rituals for the same individual on differ-ent occasions. Participants often wait until they can have maximum control over the three main structures of the ritual, which relate to surroundings, apparatus and process. Self-injury rituals can range from the relatively simple to the highly sophisticated. In terms of length of time taken to complete, they may last from a few minutes to several days. Levels of emotional intensity can vary and include both high and low periods, as can the psychological functions of the ritual which range from relief from extreme emotional distress and self- punishment to self-soothing and suicide prevention. Certain items and features involved in the process can take on additional symbolic meaning and become central characteristics of the ritual, perhaps even ends in themselves. This symbolic encapsulation can relate to blade and blood fixation in particular and can even alter meanings of everyday items used in the patching up stage.

One particularly striking observation I have made while exploring and writing about self-injury rituals concerns the effect of the ritual on the senses of the human body. The people who took part in this study have communicated deeply personal meanings held for the *sight* of blood, scars and self-injury equipment; the *touch* of the blade, pain and the softness of soothing gauze; the *sound* of emotionally evocative music, weeping and silence; the *smell* of antiseptic lotion and scented candles; and the salty *taste* of tears. The psychological benefits of the ritual have been explored and are immense. When psychological and physical senses are stimulated together as they are, one could conclude that the self-injury ritual is an extreme, but logical, form of self-help in the form of a therapeutic workout for the emotional and physical sensory systems.

6
Stigma and Damaged Lives

'Heart failure' [by Dawn]

I like cutting myself
I like having to have 'OK' clothes and clothes for when 'I hurt'
Short or long sleeve day? Hmmm?

People who begin and continue to self-injure, do so for a number of reasons, many of which are described in this book. There are, however, high social and personal costs to be contended with, not only in direct relation to the self-injury itself but also concerning the long-lasting legacy of original suffering from which self-injury can emerge. This chapter identifies costs in both of these areas and investigates how people who self-injure attempt to negotiate them. Theories of stigma and trajectory form the theoretical backdrop to a discussion focusing on how people navigate actual or expected responses to stigma and how the far-reaching consequences of original trajectory of suffering can be felt in other areas of life.

Stigma and self-injury

One of the major challenges confronting individuals who self-injure is that of stigma. Very little academic work has been carried out on stigma related to self-injury. The exceptions are Hodgson (2004), who touched upon primary stigma management strategies, and Adler and Adler (2007, 2011) who commented on stigma reduction as part of the changing social face of self-injury. These studies, as well as some which examine stigma in other realms, such as mental illness (Herman, 1986), epilepsy (Jacoby, 1994; Scambler and Hopkins, 1986), voluntary childlessness (Park, 2002), infertility (Riessman, 2000), HIV and Aids (Green and Sobo, 2000) and lesbian parenthood (Almack, 2007) have analysed and expanded earlier works, particularly the classic *Stigma: Notes on the management of spoiled identity* (Goffman, 1963) and others (Scott and Lyman, 1968; Sykes and Matza, 1957). Here I will draw on all this work. I will identify additional stigma management techniques with an emphasis on the fluidity with which they are used. I will also apply the concepts of 'felt' and 'enacted' stigmas (Scambler and Hopkins, 1986) to construct a more in-depth representation of the stigma of self-injury than has so far been articulated.

The word stigma originates from stigmata, a term used by ancient Greeks to describe the marking of the skin of slaves and criminals, by cutting or burning, to ensure they would be recognisable as defective or immoral and shunned by others in public places (Goffman, 1963). Today's sociological use of the word stigma refers to the metaphorical marking of certain individuals as shameful, dishonourable, or unworthy, based on an undesirable characteristic. For Goffman (1963), a stigma is a sign that devalues an individual's social identity so as to disqualify him/her from full social acceptability. He distinguished the difference between stigmas which are known to others (discrediting stigmas) and those which are not yet apparent to others (discreditable stigmas), and emphasised the importance for the stigmatised individual to avoid situations in which the former could occur. He further identified three forms of stigma, those of body, character and tribe. A bodily stigma becomes apparent when an individual's physical appearance is outside that which is considered 'normal' or desirable in society. Examples of this might be facial deformities, obesity or height (i.e. too short or too tall). A character or behavioural stigma implies that an individual possesses undesirable personality traits such as criminality, addiction, or mental illness and is usually perceived as weak-willed. Third, a tribal stigma can be applied to affiliation with a particular religion, race or nationality which is considered to deviate from the normative of that society, such as being Jewish in Nazi Germany, or Muslim in contemporary United States. This book is not concerned with tribal stigma. Self-injury is a phenomenon which is mainly concerned with character stigma. However, scars left by self-injury mean that categorisation can spill over into that of bodily stigma, and indeed it is often the visibility of one's scarring (whether intentionally or otherwise) that leads to the discrediting of the individual.

Many individuals, whose self-injury becomes known to 'normals' (referred to as such by Goffman (1963:5) as those others, who do not possess the stigma in question), experience discrimination. The main reason for the display of animosity directed towards people who are discredited as 'self-injurers' is noted by Page:

> Those with conduct stigmas are generally considered to be personally responsible for their failings. It is commonly believed that such individuals have deliberately chosen to behave in socially unacceptable ways. As such they are liable to be treated unfavourably by others. (1984:6)

People who self-injure are often subjected to punitive and disparaging treatment. Terms such as 'freak', 'nutter', 'attention seeker', 'suicidal', 'manipulative' and 'time waster', have been verbalised by non-self-injuring individuals to describe people who cut, burn or otherwise injure themselves. The people reported as having meted out such derogatory and unsympathetic criticism are in every section of the individuals' lives and include: family, friends, work colleagues, medical personnel and strangers.

Regardless of whether or not they consider the stigma to be justified, people who self-injure perceive self-injury as a stigmatised behaviour, a position supported by everyone who spoke to me for this book. It is important to consider how the stigmatised person assesses his or her own behaviour and that of others like them. This particular area has, in the past, been under-represented in studies of stigma, as Schneider and Conrad (1980) point out:

> Most sociological work on stigma assumes that the stigmatised learn the meaning of their attribute or performance primarily through direct exposure to rejection and disapproval from others. Less understood is the place of the *perception of stigma* – of what the putatively stigmatised think others think of them and 'their kind' and about how these others might react to disclosure. (Schneider and Conrad, 1980:35)

In a similar vein to that of Cooley's (1964) 'Looking glass self', the individual is able to imagine her or his self and her or his actions reflected and judged by society as favourable or otherwise. Scambler and Hopkins' (1986) analysis of the stigma associated with epilepsy, extending Goffman's work on stigma, focused on the importance of how the stigmatised individual identifies with the stigma. At the 'core' of their respondents' 'special view of the world' was 'their sense of epilepsy as stigma' (Scambler and Hopkins, 1986:33). These authors took Goffman's (1963:23) point that 'the very anticipation of stigmatising encounters can lead the stigmatised individual to arrange life so as to avoid them' and introduced the concepts of 'enacted' and 'felt' stigma. These concepts prove especially useful in our attempts to understand the stigma of self-injury. 'Enacted' stigma refers to encounters of negative treatment of individuals on the basis of their stigmatising attribute. 'Felt' stigma is, as Scambler and Hopkins (1986) assert, 'more complex'. This term concerns primarily, 'the fear of enacted stigma' (Scambler and Hopkins, 1986:33) and it includes the person's acceptance of the disreputable feature as shameful, whether or not they believe the shame to be valid, or a violation against what Goffman terms 'norms of identity or being' (Goffman, 1963:152; Scambler and Hopkins, 1986:33). The osmotic process of absorbing society's sense of 'normal' and 'crazy', 'acceptable' and 'unacceptable' behaviour ensures that the self-injuring individual is concerned primarily with three main factors. First, that self-injury is an unacceptable behaviour in society, and second, that disclosure of the activity will bring undesirable consequences. As most individuals who self-injure discover, indefinite concealment is often emotionally demanding and usually not practically possible as the chance of accidental disclosure is high. Third, the desire to control information about their self-injuring identity is a major goal. Whether or not their self-injury was eventually known about by family, friends, colleagues, strangers or medical personnel, all participants expressed the need, via a range of information control techniques, to reduce the likelihood of their self-injury becoming known to others, or, to minimise the discrediting effects of disclosure. They were often faced with a range of decisions in relation 'to display or not to display, to tell or not to tell, to let on or not to let on, to lie or not to lie; and in each case to whom, how, when and where' (Goffman, 1963:42).

At the time of interview, participants were asked whether or not other people knew about their self-injury. Levels of openness with others ranged from complete secrecy on one end of a sliding scale to complete transparency on the other. A small minority was located on each polar end, reporting full secrecy (no one aside from themselves knew about their self-injury) on one side and total openness (no attempt was made to hide the behaviour) on the other. Most people were positioned somewhere in the middle of the scale, affirming that their self-injury was known to a few individuals. People who knew tended to be family members or close friends, one or more work colleagues, a doctor or therapist. Some participants had made themselves and their self-injury known to users of social networking or self-injury websites. Disclosure was not necessarily intentional or consistent. Although many deliberately volunteered information (usually tentatively and based on a perceived and expected reaction) to one or more of the above individuals or groups, others gave accounts of people discovering their self-injuring upon seeing scars or refusing to accept unconvincing stories of accidental injury. In addition some of the people in whom they confided passed the information on to third parties.

Sally (a 34-year-old single woman who was sexually abused in childhood by her older brother) used the term 'cutting career' to describe significant stages in the progression of her self-injury and her own perception of the behaviour. When examining all interview transcripts for evidence of stigma, I identified a pattern of themes consistent to respondents and to which this term can be usefully applied. The concept of 'cutting career' is reminiscent of Goffman's (1963:32) 'moral career', as it takes account of the sequential characteristics of the self-injuring individual concerning both internal (e.g. relationship with self, identity etc.) and external matters (e.g. relationship with others). The term 'cutting career' in this study, however, not only refers to decisive action taken by individuals, it also includes the sense of feeling driven and controlled. Regarding external themes, encounters of 'enacted' stigma are of interest. Internal themes are concerned with changes associated with the person's level of 'felt' stigma, subsequent use of information control techniques, strategies of neutralisation and therapeutic disclosure.

The experience of negative reaction: 'enacted stigma'

Sometimes they wouldn't even anesthetise it

For the majority of people who self-injure, there eventually comes a point when their injuries become known to others as having been self-inflicted. Although there are also examples of sympathetic responses, this section deals with the negative reactions of others when self-injury is uncovered. Whether disclosure is accidental or deliberate, experiences of 'enacted stigma' as described by Scambler and Hopkins (1986) often follow. Negative encounters affect all spheres of life and involve other people, ranging from family members, friends and work colleagues to medical personnel and strangers.

Some of those who spoke to me recalled explosive rows with parents or siblings when scars were revealed as being self-inflicted or could not be plausibly explained as accidental. Eve's mother walked into her bedroom to find her cutting her arm with a piece of broken glass. Her mum's reaction was typical of many close relatives:

> She had a major rant at me. She was angry and shocked. Then she started crying and saying how it was all her fault … that she hadn't brought me up properly and that I should have been able to talk to her about my problems instead of doing this. [Eve]

In contrast to the perception of self-injury as somehow the result of their own poor parenting, other parents placed responsibility firmly with the child:

> My dad said I was a selfish, attention seeking, little bastard for doing this to him and Mum. Like I was doing this to get back at them for stuff. They couldn't understand that it was nothing to do with them. I never wanted them to know. It was meant to be private. [Tom]

Moreover, aside from the assumption that self-injury is the individual's attempt to punish or somehow control others, parents and other family members may resort to emotional pleads and/or threats:

> My sister pleaded with me 'Why are you doing this to us?' and 'Why can't you stop for us, the people who love you?'…'If you cared about us at all you'd stop hurting yourself like this'. [Aoife]

Reactions involving anger, shock, assumption, apportioning of blame, feelings of guilt and the like may be displayed in isolation. But it is important to note that the above negative responses from parents, other family members and close friends are usually not fixed or consistent. More often than not, those close to the person who self-injures will exhibit more than one of these often conflicting responses, changing between emotions, as they struggle to come to terms with the fact that their loved one has been self-injuring.

Once the initial shock of the discovery has passed, some people may resort to what are often futile attempts to prevent continuation of another's self-injury:

> I felt like I was being watched all the time…or being followed about the place. Their eyes were always on me. They would be asking where I was going, or shouting into the bathroom to see if I was OK. It was a bit suffocating to be honest. [Aoife]

In addition to being put on what can be described as self-injury watch, another technique aimed at preventing someone from self-injuring is to remove implements that he or she could use to cut or burn:

> My sister hides the knives when I'm there. I don't even use knives, I only use blades and I certainly wouldn't cut myself with her knives in her house. [Steve]

Similarly, Susan recalls her husband's reaction to seeing the scars, left by episodes of burning and cutting:

> My husband…There's no matches allowed in the house and there's no lighters allowed in the house…He checks the drawers every night in case there's matches anywhere. Obviously he can't check for everything sharp because there's always going to be sharp things about. [Susan]

Besides her example of enacted stigma, Susan has highlighted the obvious flaw in the strategies of hiding or removing, in noting the ready availability of implements which could be used for purposes of self-injury.

At times, experiences of enacted stigma are instigated when information, which was initially disclosed (voluntarily or otherwise) to one person or persons, is passed on to other people. Nora experienced negative treatment as an indirect result of disclosing her self-injury to her boyfriend. Details about her self-injury were then passed on to others, to whom Nora had no intention of telling. The result was highly undesirable and resulted in Nora losing her home:

> He [her boyfriend] went and told my girlfriend and then she told my landlord. And then it was a whole thing where he was evicting me...He [landlord] felt I was an unstable tenant to have...he finally did evict me and he said it was because I was unstable and he couldn't risk it. [Nora]

Goffman addresses the implications of close relationships on the stigmatised individual's ability to control information:

> Relationships can necessitate time spent together, and the more time the individual spends with another the more chance the other will acquire discrediting information about him. Further,...every relationship obliges the related persons to exchange an appropriate amount of intimate facts about self, as evidence of trust and mutual commitment. (Goffman, 1963:86)

Nora did not personally disclose her self-injury to the landlord. The risk involved in exposing scars to her boyfriend, within what she trusted to be the privacy of an intimate relationship, proved devastating, culminating in her eviction. Scambler and Hopkins' (1986:34) study participant usefully sums up this position in describing his experiences of stigma in relation to epilepsy: 'One person knows and tells another person, and there it is, it's like a bushfire!' (Scambler and Hopkins, 1986:34)

Aside from negative treatment from family, friends and others, one of the main sources of enacted stigma reported by those who spoke to me was the medical profession. Most people had at least one negative encounter in a medical setting. According to participants, suspected or confirmed (whether or not by the individual) self-injury was usually met with unsympathetic attitudes from a broad range of medical personnel. These included staff (both doctors and nurses) in accident and emergency departments and those who came in contact with people who self-injure in the fields of psychiatry and counselling. Disparaging treatment was also received from staff in medical settings unrelated to self-injury. Sally recalls negative treatment received when her self-injury was suspected by nurses and a doctor during a medical examination related to her physical disability. She describes how she felt on this occasion:

> They seem to think it's acceptable to sit in the corner and talk about me. I heard them whispering, 'Did you see the marks on her arm?' Everyone in the room could hear them and I remember feeling like a freak. [Sally]

The impact of assumptions of time wasting, attention seeking, suicidal ideation and psychiatric disorder can have severe detrimental effects on people who self-injure and will be discussed further in relation to felt stigma below. Among some of the most acute examples of enacted stigma by medical personnel reported was the stitching of cuts without the use of anaesthetic. One such experience recalled by Steve is representative of other similar accounts reported:

> STEVE: I avoid going to A&E … when you went to the hospital you knew you were left outside longer than you should have been. You were brought in and um … you could hear the innuendos flying … You know 'Oh, we've a live one in there' …. 'There's a self-harmer in …'
>
> THERESA: Were these psychiatric staff?
>
> STEVE: No just ordinary nursing staff and doctors at A&E … And they would ask 'Oh why did you do that?' And 'Right let's have a look at that'. And 'Right someone will be in shortly to deal with that'. Of course then, after another long wait, someone comes in and pours something that stings the brains out of you

and starts stitching you up. Some of them can be really heavy handed. Sometimes they wouldn't even anaesthetise it. You got the odd one who was sympathetic...Not that you were looking for sympathy anyway...But not some nurse who wanted to add to the pain and humiliation you already felt...And then you were sent away and that was that.

THERESA: How did that treatment make you feel?

STEVE: Angry...really angry...Like I was a second-hand citizen. [Steve]

'Long sleeves and stories of cats scratching'. The fear of negative reaction: 'felt stigma'

The concept of felt stigma (Scambler and Hopkins, 1986) was introduced above and in many ways is more involved and complicated than the idea of enacted stigma. As argued by Goffman (1963), stigmatised individuals may accept society's opinion of their conduct that labels them as possessing a dishonourable feature. Many individuals, like Tina (a 39-year-old housewife), internalised society's opinion of self-injury as a shameful behaviour long before she was subjected to any negative treatment from others:

I would feel so guilty afterwards [after self-injuring]...so ashamed of myself because I knew it was wrong, but I couldn't help myself. I just had to do it and then live with myself afterwards. [Tina]

In addition to feeling ashamed of the behaviour, the fear of undesirable reactions from others was at the forefront of Nora's felt stigma:

...the implications of people finding out then just became so scary to me...you know...what if my family find out?...what if my friends find out?...the ones in work?...I'm going to lose my job...I'm gonna get locked up...that was a big thing, that I'm gonna get locked up and everyone is going to know I'm so crazy. [Nora]

For most of the study participants, the main goal in the early stages of the 'cutting career' was disclosure avoidance, due to their fear of a negative reaction from others. Usually, the first technique used in what becomes a sequence of managing stigma is that of 'passing'. 'Passing' is a primary 'information control' technique whereby individuals endeavour to hide their stigmatised feature (Goffman, 1963). According to Goffman, the desire to appear 'normal' is what prompts people who are in a position to 'pass' to do so. 'Passing' was most often accomplished, by all participants in this study, by choosing to self-injure in places where cuts and scars could be easily hidden from the view of others, for example, under long sleeves. Anne, a 19-year-old student who was sexually abused, recalls 'passing' her scars:

> Well, when I started, I cut my lower arms on the inside and on my upper left arm. And because I was at school I was wearing a uniform anyway. And it was winter coming into spring, so it was OK. And…um…they left small marks and um…the marks were never very big, cus the razor was very thin so it left very thin lines…it sort of progressed to different places where people wouldn't see because I didn't want it to be seen…So I'd use my upper legs and stomach. [Anne]

Like Anne, most of the participants, including Dawn, a 21-year-old student who was invalidated at home by her parents and bullied at school, were caught between the relief felt when she cut herself and a strong awareness of the unacceptability of the behaviour:

> I felt better after [self-injuring] and then about ten minutes later I started to feel bad about it, cos I thought 'God, I have to go and cover this up now'. You knew, that was you having to wear long sleeves for the next week. [Dawn]

Almack (2007), in her discussion of the stigma of lesbian parenthood, develops the concept of 'passing' further, arguing that the technique is not as 'static' as Goffman proposed. She asserts that 'avoidance can be a fluid rather than a fixed response, used some of the time and in some circumstances' (Almack, 2007:8.1). This fluidity is evident in the case of Susan, a 44-year-old married mother of four. Due to her fear of negative reaction, Susan's day-to-day living usually involved concealing her self-injury from all but immediate family members. Her husband and teenage sons knew she cut and burned herself and while they had individually and collectively expressed a number of the emotions described above, they were simultaneously concerned for Susan in their efforts to understand and support her. While shopping in a supermarket on a foreign holiday with her family, the scars on her arm were noticed by the shop owner. He shook his finger and his head at Susan and in broken English admonished her for her self-injury and told her not to do it again. Susan chose not to 'pass' her scars while on holiday. She made the decision under the influence of the prevailing situation in which she found herself. The particularly hot weather conditions combined with the temporary nature of her relationship with people she would encounter so far from home prompted Susan to risk stigmatising treatment.

> I was so embarrassed. I wanted the ground to swallow me up. But I suppose it was my own fault. I was on holiday so I weighed it up in my mind and took a risk. It was such a hot day so I decided not to cover up as much as I usually do back at home. And I thought, 'Well, sure I'll never have to see anyone I meet here again'. [Susan]

Back at home and in different circumstances (e.g. at her place of work) Susan was much more likely to 'pass' her self-injury by hiding the evidence under clothing, even during hot weather.

Difficulties associated with hiding injuries can lead to incidents in which they are inadvertently discovered, and 'passing' techniques progress to 'cover stories' (Hodgson, 2004). 'Covering', according to Goffman (1963) is the technique of presenting a socially acceptable explanation to reduce stigma. Hodgson's (2004) self-injuring respondents revealed the use of this method which involved the fabrication of plausible accounts, of scars being the result of accidents with pets, or while cooking. The participants of this study produced numerous cover stories. Nora, a 30-year-old laboratory technician who was raped in her early twenties, was motivated to cover her self-injury, because of the fear of how others would react. She capitalised on her use of blades in her daily work-life to devise a believable cover story when her mother noticed a scar:

> I didn't want people to know cus I was scared of the reaction. I was obsessed with getting locked up. I made up stories. My mum said to me when she saw a cut on my arm and I told her I got it in

work...That was the only time I made up a story cus most of the time the cuts were well hidden. [Nora]

Marie (a 27-year-old who was sexually abused in childhood by three different individuals on separate occasions) recalled using a variety of cover stories:

THERESA: What about family and friends? Did you take any pre-cautions to keep secrets from them or did you maybe hide cuts?

MARIE: Yea I would have cut myself in places where no one would see it and I would have made up stories about them.

THERESA: What kind of stories would you have made up?

MARIE: Um...I poured a kettle over my arm by mistake. The dog tripped me up into the window, so the dog got the blame. Um...the dog gave me a black eye, burst lip...um...I was looking for the cat and I cut my leg on wire. Um...What else was there...I cut my face when I was wakening up. The alarm went off and I cut my face on the bedside cabinet. [Marie]

Many participants described their self-injury as neat, controlled cuts, which sometimes could not be successfully explained by conventional accounts of mishaps. On these occasions, individuals were often 'outed' as having caused the injuries themselves. Others, however, were undeterred in this regard and may have changed their method of injury as a strategy to cover more successfully:

I'd just get out an iron, or hair-straighteners, cos I have those at my disposal. And it looks more like an accident than cutting. So I could still get away with people thinking it was an accident. [Dawn]

Sally's felt stigma was so strong that on the one occasion when she was required to undergo a medical examination she gave an alias. She describes her motivation for passing herself under a false identity:

It was (a) self-preservation because they couldn't trace me to lock me up. And (b) they couldn't put it on my medical file. And I was glad I lied because if you don't you have to take the punishment. I created my own personal identity because I was so frightened. [Sally]

During a previous experience, while taking part in a counselling session regarding sexual abuse, Sally was threatened with forced hospital admission if she were to cut herself again. This led her to believe that by creating a false identity she could avoid being labelled as mentally ill on her medical notes and avoid the risk of being formally detained under mental health legislation. She could not however escape being subjected to 'enacted' stigma in the form of the disparaging medical treatment she received. She recalled that staff were judgemental and made her feel 'like a freak', embarrassed and ashamed. Sally's treatment at the hands of medical staff aroused emotions that she recalled as similar to those experienced in childhood. Not only did she remember feeling that she was 'bad' but also that she did not have permission to speak to the nurses and doctors about why she had cut herself:

I felt like I was 16 again. I felt the judgement, the disapproval, the fear, the humiliation of being told 'That's a very silly thing to do. You'll not do that again in a hurry'. No one wanted to know why I did it...Just stitch her up and throw her out. [Sally]

Most of the study participants exhibited similar levels of felt stigma and many remarked that a little understanding for people who self-injure would go a long way in alleviating suffering in those who self-injure. Individuals vested with the power to alleviate suffering, including close family members, friends and medical personnel, can sometimes contribute to a worsening of the situation. This sentiment is reflected in wider literature from the perspective of the individual (Johnstone, 1997). Many people who self-injure expect negative reactions from medical staff and may avoid seeking treatment for their injuries, unless the wound(s) is (are) severe. Most wounds are self-managed. The stigmatising effect of being branded a 'cutter', a time waster, an attention seeker and undeserving of respect or compassion has a detrimental effect on the individual's identity. Often the stigma of self-injury promotes a self-fulfilling prophesy, which may lead to continued and often worsened self-injury. Mike (a 40-year-old clergyman who was abused in childhood by three different individuals on separate occasions) illustrates this point by recalling how he was treated when he sought professional help in relation to his self-injury:

> He [his psychotherapist] was punitive in his approach. He was intimidatory. He was aggressive towards me and frightened me. He sometimes mocked me…You know, 'You're feeling sorry for yourself. Pull yourself together.' And I was so bad one night after one of his sessions, I self-harmed that night'. [Mike]

The viewpoint of self-injury as manipulative and attention seeking has been noted as permitting those in charge of delivering therapeutic and medical treatments to validate minimalist attention, rationalised by the behaviourist principle of positive and negative reinforcement of not 'rewarding' the behaviour (Johnstone, 1997; Pembroke, 1994; Solomon and Farrand, 1996).

Long sleeves and stories of scratching cats, as well as the employment of strategies for ensuring self-injuries looked accidental, proved, in the beginning for most, effective techniques in preventing disclosure and for presenting self-injury scars in a socially acceptable format. For many of this study's participants these techniques were sufficient ways to maintain what Goffman (1963) refers to as a 'discreditable' (their social stigma is not readily identifiable or known about) identity in social interactions with others for many years.

Passing and covering are effective techniques for dealing with felt stigma and continue to be useful in social interactions with the uninformed. Once the behaviour of self-injury is actually out and known about, new tactics are required. Being revealed as a 'self-injurer' requires alternative strategies to be used in front of audiences who are 'in the know'. At this stage in the 'cutting career', the priority becomes the minimisation or neutralisation of the stigma via the technique of accounting. 'Accounts' are statements that justify or excuse the unacceptable behaviour once it has been exposed (Hodgson, 2004; Mills, 1940; Scott and Lyman, 1968). They are used at this stage 'to tell people about the behaviour on their own terms' (Hodgson, 2004:173) to make it sound more socially acceptable. The information is out, so it might as well be presented in the best possible light.

Examples of accounts are many and varied. Most of the people who spoke to me cited negative childhood experiences as being at the root of their self-injury. A few blamed themselves for past events. Nora, for example, felt responsible for the death of her childhood friend in an accident involving them both. She self-injured as a way to 'punish' herself as well as to 'get rid of anxiety'. Among those who gave accounts of negative experiences in childhood, blame for self-injury was more often placed onto others. The depositing of responsibility onto people who were deemed at fault for childhoods in which the individuals felt generally invalidated was common. A recurrent account involved the failure of adults to teach 'healthy' ways of dealing with emotions, again implying that others were to blame. Tina charged others in both of these ways:

> In our house you weren't allowed to express any negative emotions. If you cried in front of my Ma or Da you were told to 'wise up' and 'don't be so bloody dramatic'. I was never taught to deal with emotions. You just had to hold them in…but they had to come out somewhere…and then I just started to cut them out. [Tina]

Blaming abusers was common among individuals who had been sexually and/or physically and/or emotionally abused, as was the case with Lisa (a 28-year-old single woman):

> I'm usually thinking of the abuse when I'm cutting myself…I have thoughts of my cousin [abuser] when I see the blood being released. The blood gets rid of the bad feeling. [Lisa]

Many who were abused expressed a need to have someone listen to their experiences but felt unable to share the information with others. The reasons given for this inability to communicate were mainly in regard to shame associated with sexual abuse, and/or because of fear (actual or imagined) that no one would believe them, and/or because of threats of ill-treatment. Lena, a 28-year-old single unemployed woman who was sexually abused in a children's institution and also by her brother-in-law, illustrates this point:

LENA: When I was twelve he started coming round to my school...to threaten me...He would say 'I'm really sorry, but if you tell anyone I'll kill you'.

THERESA: Did you tell anyone?

LENA: Eventually, yes...my sister.

THERESA: How did she react?

LENA: She said I was making it up. She said he was a good and holy man and she beat me up...but I went to the police then. I told them what had happened and they went after him but he denied it and he got away with it...And that's when I started self-injuring...I felt like I had to cut the bad stuff away. [Lena]

Besides negative childhood experiences which are used to focus blame on oneself, but more often other people, other possible accounting strategies to minimise the stigma of self-injury involve professional diagnoses, especially in relation to mental health and disorder. Herman (1993), in her study examining the stigma associated with the re-integration of ex-psychiatric patients into the community, noticed that many used 'medical disclaimers' as an effective technique of blame avoidance, associated with psychiatric hospitalisation:

Such interpretations 'don't blame me, blame my genes!' were often used by ex-patients to evoke sympathy from others and to ensure that they would be treated in a charitable manner...through the use of medical disclaimers, ex-patients hoped to elevate their self-esteem and to renegotiate personal perceptions of mental illness as a non-stigmatising attribute. (Herman, 1993:300)

Likewise, Eve capitalised on her medical diagnosis of 'clinical depression' and pointed to a possible genetic cause of her problems and subsequent self-injury:

I must say...looking back, I wonder how much of this is genetic. My father's mother had schizophrenia and his brother was institutionalised. [Eve]

Many people who come into contact with psychiatrists in relation to self-injury may be informed that they have a mental disorder and in this study, 'borderline personality disorder', 'depression', 'bipolar' and 'psychotic' were some of the diagnoses mentioned. Although some found such psychiatric labels offensive, others used their history of psychiatric treatment and/or diagnoses as medical disclaimers in a similar fashion to that of Herman's respondents. Anne, for example, welcomed her official diagnosis, drawing on it to explain her actions and to somehow disown or deflect responsibility:

> He [psychiatrist] said that, um, I had a borderline personality disorder. I mean it does explain a lot of the things I feel. I can see myself in…I mean I read up on it after and I can see myself in a lot of it…I mean obviously not everything. I wouldn't jump to diagnosing myself to something. Sometimes it just helps to have a name, to know that you're just not making it up. That's what I always wanted, just let me know that I'm not some whiney, attention seeking, liar. [Anne]

Damaged lives

It is fair to say that self-injury is socially and personally costly to people who practise it. Following on from the direct discussion on stigma, the discussion now turns to some of the other costs incurred by people who self-injure. The main feature uniting all participants of this study, apart from self-injury, is the fact that they have all endured suffering. Riemann and Schütze (2005) identified ways in which the dynamics of the 'trajectory' of suffering continues to cause problems in many areas, even when the original source of distress no longer exists. Their position on this matter is worth quoting at length as many of the points are relevant to individuals who self-injure and to the discussion in this chapter:

> There can be still unnoticed outer forces of the trajectory potential and side effects of the fight against the trajectory dynamics. What is also very important: The trajectory incumbent has been severely afflicted by the workings of the trajectory dynamics, this changes features of her/his identity and hence, again she/he might not fit into her/his new life situation. The person can

be severely exhausted up to the point of a burn-out, and then there is no energy left for managing the new life situation. She/he might be covered by emotional, social or bodily scars and stigmas stemming from the wounds of the trajectory experience; the afflicted person and/or fellow-interactants could then be hyper-focused on these scars and they might not be able to appreciate the new positive qualities of life. The person might have felt extremely neglected by other people during the trajectory experience, and, hence, even now she or he keeps the attitude of total self-isolation as a strategy of (inadequate) reaction to it which might cause new difficulties for her or him. (Riemann and Schütze, 2005:135)

I hope, in the discussion so far, that I have been able to communicate a sense of the complex and multi-layered qualities of self-injury as part of a wider 'trajectory' of suffering. In discussing the long-term legacy of the 'trajectory', I realise that consequences can be felt in many areas of one's life which may overlap with each other and cannot easily be separated into neat compartments for isolated discussion. Bearing this understanding in mind, I do feel, however, that for the sake of clarity and ease of explanation, it is possible to view what people have told me about their suffering by focusing on three broad areas of life. For simplicity's sake I will discuss these areas under the terms: 'social paralysis', 'relationship problems' and 'vulnerability' even though I do not intend these categories to be taken as rigid factions.

Social paralysis

Wring it out and leave it dripping

Even when the original source of the suffering has ceased to be active, the disposition with which individuals experience the everyday world around them can been still sensitive to the destructive force of the trajectory. As a result, many cannot enjoy as full and active a lifestyle as they otherwise might have had. Sally, who enjoyed swimming in childhood prior to being sexually abused by her older brother, commented on how she avoided swimming pools due to shame associated with the extensive scarring on her body:

> I haven't been swimming since I started self-injuring. I just couldn't take people staring at my scars and judging me, so that's just another area of my life that's been affected. [Sally]

The socially paralysing legacy of the trajectory of suffering for many is far reaching, as exemplified by Lena. Her sexually abusive brother-in-law presented himself to the outside world as an upstanding and devout Christian. Behind closed doors, however, the religious undertones of his sexual fantasies were played out as he sexually abused Lena. Her suffering was further intensified by the fact that he used her hearing impairment as an additional means to control her:

> He was very involved with the church. He used to go to healings where they would all pray…. And have the priest over for dinner and be involved in loads of stuff in the church…. giving out communion…. They used to try and fix my ears…. And because there was so many people in the house I used to pass out and they thought that this was the healing working but it was because I was too warm and couldn't breathe….He had an altar full of candles and holy pictures in my bedroom and after he abused me he used to make me kneel down and pray for my sins to be forgiven and hold a crucifix to my ears. He said that I couldn't hear because I wasn't sorry enough…. And that God thought I didn't deserve to hear…. When I tried to tell my sister about the abuse he said I was making Jesus cry with my lies…. [Lena]

Lena revealed that she had not 'set foot inside a church', since she 'got free of him'. Damage inflicted on her religious identity spoiled any chance of the comfort and support she may have gained from a spiritual faith. Avoidance of religion and religious symbols, for Lena, was analogous with avoidance of horrific reminders of sexual abuse.

Reminders of suffering can sometimes be found in everyday objects. Ella avoids wearing certain items of clothing because they prompt memories of sexual abuse at the hands of her father:

> If I even see pleated skirts, I go haywire inside because he would abuse me when I was wearing my school uniform. I get panicky, sweaty, not being able to breath. I haven't worn skirts in I don't know how long...Probably since I left school.... [Ella]

Twenty-three years since her sexually abusive father died and the abuse ended, Ella regularly suffers from 'flashbacks', during which she is forced to remember and re-experience traumatic events. As well as skirts, she avoids drying her hair with a towel, as doing so reminds her of her father which could lead to a subsequent episode of self-injury:

> She [her mother] would always send him up to dry my hair...cus my hair was down to here [points to the bottom of her back] you know?...And to this day and I'm 39...See a towel over my head I can't have it...When I wash my hair now, I just wring it out and leave it dripping. [Ella]

Sam (a 42-year-old sales manager) endured physical neglect in childhood. He is aware of his tendency to over compensate for previous suffering by his obsessive washing of both himself and his own children:

> Also, I'm a real clean freak. I'm really fussy about keeping myself clean...and even more so when it comes to the kids. They always have to be turned out perfectly. I find myself getting upset if they're dirty...Not letting them out of the house until I have inspected them. I don't want people thinking bad of them. I think it stems back to wetting the bed when I was a kid. We [Sam and his siblings] all wet the bed and when we told my ma about it she'd just shout up the stairs, 'Just pull the sheet off the bed and turn the mattress over'. The wet sheets would lie on the floor and be put back on the bed, by us kids, when they had dried. My sisters all had long hair which would be soaked in urine come morning. We were just sent out to school like that. Needless to say we were bullied and called 'Smelly' and 'Pissy breath' and stuff. With my own kids...my wife had to stop me...I was smothering them in soap and washing them too much all the time. I think I was overly clean which I suppose isn't good either. Jenny [Sam's wife]

would say that I was going to wash all the natural oils out of their skin and that I was over the top. [Sam]

Sam also recalled feelings of anxiety and frustration on family holidays, when he became obsessed about his children getting dirty, while playing in sand. The paralysing legacy of the previous neglectful relationship hampered the ease with which he could relax and enjoy his relationship with his wife and children. Sam realised, with the support of his wife, that his excessive use of soap on his children was potentially harmful, not only to the condition of their skin but also to their psychological development and harmonious relationships within his household. For many in this study, however, relationships with other people, especially family members and spouses, were deeply imbued with a range of problems.

Relationship problems

What's he doing up there?

Everyone who spoke to me revealed relationship problems to varying degrees. People with whom relationships were affected were family members, partners, friends and work colleagues. Ella recalled how sexual abuse hampered any chance of a playful, light-hearted relationship with her brother. In one instance, he tried to surprise her by sneaking up behind her at the kitchen sink. She reacted by screaming at her brother and physically attacking him. She disclosed during the interview that her father's sexual advances were often made at her from behind as she stood washing dishes. Her brother recoiled in confusion and as Ella did not explain her extreme reaction, the relationship between them both remained damaged.

THERESA: How did your brother react?
ELLA: He backed off. He thinks I'm a psycho. [Ella]

The encounter between Ella and her brother left the relationship damaged to a certain degree. However, others reported that sibling attachment was prevented from forming at all due to factors such as childhood separation or other divisiveness within the family unit. Some people avoided siblings, because contact with brothers and sisters was a reminder of periods of severe distress. Steve gives an example:

> We were all split up from an early age and have no real bonds with each other now. I'm not really interested now, because all they want to do when we're together is to rake over old coals…and talk about our mother and stuff. [Steve]

Occasions that compel family members to spend time together can be upsetting. The release of negative emotions that had become unbearable for Steve further ostracised him from his family:

> After the funeral [his mother's] we were all in her house and my sister asked me if I wanted anything to remember her by. I blew like a fuse and I said, 'I want fuck all from her!' I really cracked up. 'What would I want to remember that parasite for? Go and buy a bottle of whiskey. That'll remind me of her'. It was my anger from the way she was. Not knowing her, from being in the homes [children's residential institutions], being abused, being treated like shit…Just the anger all built up and I self-harmed that day. And to the rest of the family I was a bastard. [Steve]

Revelations about abuse can also drive a wedge between family members. Tracey was blamed for explosive rows and divided loyalties that resulted in 'splitting the family'. When her overdose resulted in intervention from social workers, she reported her sexually abusive father to the authorities. Lack of evidence resulted in no action being taken against him, which contributed to estranged relations and more self-injury:

> I ended up going home and I just cut away at my stomach…cus I just couldn't cry. Everything was just built up inside because of the pain and…that nothing had happened [her father was not held accountable for the abuse] and I thought it was still my fault…I was the one who had done everything on the family…after the [court] case was over everybody separated…everyone was going away and I wished I hadn't spoke…wished I hadn't said anything…wished I had just let things go on…and just done what my sisters had done…got pregnant and left the house…. [Tracey]

When sexual abuse by a parent is reported to a significant other (i.e. the other parent) and is allowed to continue, further breakdown of relationships of trust can often result. Ella described feeling 'let down' and 'confused' when her mother 'turned a blind eye' to the sexual abuse:

> ...And I used to think, 'She knows he's doing it, so why is she getting him to dry my hair?'...Even after I told my ma and she yelled at him, she still left him alone with me to dry my hair.... [Ella]

In addition to relationship problems concerning parents and siblings, the ability to form and maintain relationships, outside the family of origin, presented significant difficulties for many, especially concerning issues of trust. Ella's trajectory has infiltrated so deeply into her relationships with men that her marriage and subsequent partnerships have been deeply affected:

> It caused the breakup of my marriage. Then I lived with a fella and every time he went up the stairs I was going, 'What's he doing up there? Why's he talking to the kids?' And I would go into the room after him...I have three sons now, all grown up. My partner even said to me once, 'Were you abused?' and I would always say 'No I wasn't'. I just don't trust men at all. I don't trust friend's husbands...don't trust brother-in-laws cus the way I look at it, it only takes a minute...for them to do something and that's it...someone's life is destroyed.... [Ella]

As well as her inability to trust her partner not to sexually abuse her children, Ella also speaks of her lack of sexual enjoyment and her dependency on alcohol, in preparation for intercourse:

> I started drinking alcohol when I had to have sex and it was to numb it out...And that's the way it is up to this very day...And I don't even like drink...I'd have to drink the whole bottle of vodka to get out of it and have any kind of intimate relationship with a man. [Ella]

Nora, who was raped four years prior to the interview, reported how the negative impact of the ordeal had a lasting effect on her ability to attain sexual fulfilment:

I still have flashbacks and I have to deal with that and having a boyfriend…. It's like there's a third person in the relationship…. [Nora]

Another problem identified in relation to sexual relationships concerns the impact of the self-injury itself and is one from which three observations can be made. First, fear of negative reaction at the sight of scars, or felt stigma can lead some individuals to avoid intimate relationships. Second, apprehension about the emotional effects of disclosure for the other person may compel the self-injuring individual to cease cutting or burning themselves while engaging in such a relationship. And third, resentment is sometimes felt towards the partner, who may now be seen as an obstacle to self-injury. Anne, a 19-year-old student who was bullied at school illustrates these points:

Well because of the places where I would cut, um someone who you would be with in a um, sort of very close relationship sort of sexual relationship would see. So…and you know…and the time when they would see these things it would be a horrible thing to see, if that makes any sense. So you might just avoid it [sexual intercourse]. Whenever you're close to someone, intimate and then to see your body is covered in scars and marks and stuff, you just…it's not fair on someone else because it was my way of coping and I remember thinking at one point 'God I hate the fact that because of you I can't do this'. [Anne]

Of the unattached people who spoke to me, single status was sometimes reported as being through personal choice. Having been hurt by others in the past, many preferred to avoid new relationships, not only with sexual partners but friendships in general. The technique of self-isolation to avoid being hurt by others is exemplified by Tracey, who felt that tattoos and weight gain helped her build an invisible wall around herself, as protection against further painful associations with others:

Yea…when I got the first one [tattoo], I felt big…I felt better…I just felt strong, like a different person…because I'd put on a bit of weight then and the more tattoos I got, the better I felt and everybody was afraid of me…it kept people away from me…I didn't want people near me because it was the same my whole life. I didn't want people near me. I didn't want people touching me or knowing anything about me…I'm afraid to get too close to people. [Tracey]

Further problems which develop as offshoots of the original trajectory of suffering can affect not only the life of the individual but also his or her significant other (Riemann and Schütze, 2005). Steve's wife left him to begin a new relationship with one of his friends. Although he indicated that she was initially 'understanding' and sympathetic in relation to his suffering and self-injury, she may, in the end, have become so exhausted, due to the requirement of having to constantly care for and support her troubled husband, that she was drawn into a harsh trajectory of her own. She subsequently left Steve for a relationship in which she was not required to input such a high level of emotional caretaking:

THERESA: How long were you married?
STEVE: I was with her for 13 years and married for six of them. She was very understanding and we got on really well…. She just didn't love me anymore…I just put it down to that. And there was a third party involved. It was one of my friends got divorced and called to the house a lot to talk about it and he took her away from me. I self-harmed a lot then. That was a really bad time. [Steve]

Vulnerability

Multi-impulsive bulimic associated with alcohol, sex, food and self-injury

The final section in this chapter on the costs associated with self-injury deals with ways in which the original trajectory can leave the individual who self-injures vulnerable to additional self-harming behaviours and, if they have been sexually abused, to further abuse and sexual exploitation. Over half of this study's participants revealed that they had been sexually abused. Problems with consensual sexual relationships in later life have been discussed. For a number in this group, however, sexual abuse and sexual exploitation continued. Lena reported being abused by older boys while she was resident in a children's residential home. She had also suffered in a similar way at the hands of her brother-in-law. Mike was abused by three 'family friends' on separate occasions during childhood. Marie (a 27-year-old, unemployed, married woman) and Lisa (a 28-year-old, unemployed, single woman) were abused by three different individuals in childhood. Mike offered his thoughts on recurrent sexual abuse in an individual's life involving more than one abuser:

> I think men who would do those things to a child [sexual abuse] ... I think they can sense the vulnerable kids ... They're a bit like sharks who can smell blood from far off ... the easy target gives off an air of vulnerability I suppose and over a childhood a vulnerable kid is likely gona bump into more than one of these guys. [Mike]

Vulnerability to sexual exploitation in adulthood was observed in some of the people who spoke to me. Molly, for example, was drawn into a cycle of illicit sexual relationships with a number of married men. As a result of unprotected sexual intercourse with these men, she on occasion became pregnant, suffered miscarriage and had three abortions. Molly also experienced altercations with some of her lovers' spouses, which in more than one instance descended into violence.

For some people, self-injury is their only method of self-harm. It is not unusual, however, for others to use it alongside additional forms, a position supported in wider literature (Arnold and Magill, 2000). A trajectory of suffering involving self-injury can involve a progression onto one or more other forms of self-harm such as alcohol and drug abuse, eating disorders and general unhealthy or risk-taking lifestyles. Fifteen out of the twenty-five people who took part in this study revealed problems related to drug and /or alcohol abuse. Tracey recalls being introduced to alcohol at an early age:

> ... The main thing I remember was ... it sticks in my head was the time I tried to leave the house. I was about 20 and Tommy [her father] had my Ma up against the wall by the throat and was trying to strangle her and said that I wasn't leaving the house ... I ended up staying. I thought he was going to kill her ... The two of them just used to be apart and you had to take one side or the

other side. I was the one that used to sit with my ma while she drank. I used to sit and drink a bottle of cider while she drank 'Pernod'. I first started drinking when I started secondary school so I would have been 11. [Tracey]

Many participants who had abused alcohol moved on to drug use. Of these individuals, misuse of painkillers and prescription medication such as tranquilisers was common. A few like Tracey, however, progressed even further into illicit drug use:

We [Tracey and partner] would have both sat and drank and injected ourselves. So I was cutting myself and for a long time also abusing alcohol and drugs. [Tracey]

Eating disorders were also disclosed. Steve was one of the twelve individuals to reveal bulimia or anorexia. He reported that during 'extremely stressful' periods, he would 'stop eating' and 'lose a lot of weight'. Some described how they would alternate between bulimic or anorexic periods and episodes of self-injury. Self-injury seemed to lessen a desire for other forms of self-harm. Rachel, who was rejected by her father in childhood, notes different purposes served by alternative methods of self-harm:

THERESA: What about the difference between bulimia and self-injury?

RACHEL: I think they serve the same purpose but they are different in the way you feel afterwards...with the self-harm it was a distraction in that I was really upset about something and I had something else to focus on...but with the bulimia after I was sick I just felt so much better...I think they were both a release in some way...I felt like I had kind of got rid of everything with the bulimia whereas cutting was a distraction.

Another commonly expressed problem for this study's participants was (often unwelcome) psychiatric attention and diagnoses. Twenty-one respondents revealed diagnoses including, 'borderline personality disorder' and 'bipolar disorder'. Moreover, some had been hospitalised in relation to drug overdoses or eating disorders.

Molly's medical definition encompasses some self-harming behaviours which can additionally beset people who self-injure. During a period of hospitalisation in an eating disorder hospital in England, she was diagnosed as a 'multi-impulsive bulimic associated with alcohol, sex, food and self-injury'.

A final vulnerability was that of the tendency for a small minority of participants to engage in illegal or socially deviant behaviour, in addition to sexual promiscuity already discussed. Tom's uncle murdered his grandfather and aunt when Tom was ten years old. Later he engaged in high risk taking activities, such as driving at high speeds and climbing dangerous heights. He also recalled being the victim of violence:

> I was singled out for being different. I was 18 and I was out late on my own one night. And I suppose I asked for it by walking through that area. I got beat up by _____ [name of paramilitary organisation] and was in hospital for ages…I still get migraines and nose bleeds and have problems with my memory. [Tom]

Tracey maintained that if she hadn't had 'such a shit childhood', she would never have taken the drastic steps that she took, which ended in her serving a term in prison for criminal activity:

> I've always felt like an evil person…I've always felt like I'm really bad all through secondary school…you know after I found out [that her relationship with her father was termed sexual abuse]…the way I got on in there. I started smoking. I started drinking. I started taking stuff. Then I was just always putting myself down as being bad…when I threw the petrol over Tommy's [her father] door and I ended up in prison. [Tracey]

It is clear that the lives of people who self-injure can be negatively impacted in many areas. The main discussion in this chapter has focused on stigma. Examples of enacted stigma are many and varied. More complex, however, is the fear of negative reaction and the ways in which people who self-injure develop a range of techniques to avoid, reduce and manage stigma. The far-reaching effects of the original trajectory of suffering can pervade many areas of life with long-term effects. Inability to function satisfactorily in daily life, or to enjoy life to as full a capacity as might have been otherwise possible, had the individual not been caught up in a trajectory of suffering, has been demonstrated in the three broad and overlapping spheres of relationship problems, social paralysis and 'vulnerability' to further suffering.

7
Disclosure, Redefinition and Resilience

'Eclipse' [by Dawn]

This effort is overwhelming me
This effort I find tough to sustain
A happy disposition.

I am old enough to choose
This is a task I am failing in
And I yearn for a relapse.

Already thinking of reasons, of excuses
But I don't need any.

I am alive, and sometimes,
Sometimes
To me
That is pain enough to not require a reason.

I remember that dragonfly we saw in the field
The blazing heat
The warm sun.

My life has happy times.

People who self-injure can go to great lengths to keep the behaviour hidden from others. It is frequently the case, however, that self-injury will eventually be exposed. We have already examined some negative reactions encountered when self-injury is (often unintentionally) revealed. Even after successfully hiding evidence of cutting or burning, sometimes for many years, people may intentionally disclose the information to others. Keeping self-injury a secret indefinitely can be both physically and emotionally draining. When revealed voluntarily, it is often only done so to individuals who are deemed trustworthy and from whom a sympathetic reaction is expected. The process of discussing one's self-injury, including its origins and continued use, in a supportive environment can prove beneficial. In addition to the initial relief one may feel upon offloading guarded information onto someone else, sharing one's difficulties can create opportunities for change. Although some people begin to self-reflect independently of others, such discussions can help to open up possibilities for new perspectives on one's situation and the potential to increase control in one's environment. Change becomes possible not only in terms of one's external state of affairs but also internally concerning his or her assessment of self-injury and life circumstances. Techniques of accounting to self and others, which were introduced in the previous chapter, can aid people to redefine their situations into narratives which make their own suffering more tolerable and self-injury more acceptable in wider society. The purpose of techniques of accounting used by those who self-injure is to lessen the damaging effects of their own experiences on themselves and to redefine self-injury in order for society to understand it as something other than a behaviour which deserves to be stigmatised. Drawing again on theories of stigma and trajectory, the aim of this chapter is to examine how people endeavour to redefine, control and escape their suffering.

Therapeutic disclosures

There were no threats, no disapproving looks, no assumptions

Hodgson (2004:175), in describing the manner in which her respondents made their self-injury known to others, stated that 'disclosure often came in small steps as participants told trusted friends or family members and gradually stopped hiding'. While this author presents disclosure as a continuous process, from secrecy to openness in all circles of relations with other people, it is not always as straightforward, measured or deliberate as the quote may imply. Many people will eventually tell another person or persons about their self-injury.

The focus of this section is the therapeutic value of revealing information about one's self-injury to others. A small minority of participants in this study reached a stage of blanket disclosure, when, like Tina, they stopped hiding scars and making up stories to minimise stigma:

> I got to the point when I thought 'Fuck you! I'm sick of hiding'. I just couldn't do it anymore...all the lies and stuff. [Tina]

Others had had their self-injury discovered accidentally, by family members, friends, colleagues or strangers, who, as discussed in the previous chapter, often reacted unfavourably. Most who voluntarily told others about their self-injury did so in a measured manner which depended largely upon the audience. The main purpose of voluntary disclosure is therapeutic. According to Herman (1993:309):

> Therapeutic disclosure can be defined as the selective disclosure of a discreditable attribute to certain 'trusted', 'empathetic' supportive others in an effort to renegotiate personal perceptions of the stigma of 'failing'.

Disclosure as therapy has been highlighted not only in the study of ex-psychiatric patients (Herman, 1993) but also in other stigmatising situations, such as epilepsy (Schneider and Conrad, 1980) and involuntary childlessness in women (Miall, 1989). Similarities between these social realms and self-injury can be identified regarding the advantages of confiding with other people. Disclosure can prove beneficial in relieving the tiring and demanding work concerned with keeping self-injury hidden. Many people who self-injure report liberating effects involved in telling someone else:

> It was amazing. Someone else actually knew about what I had been doing to myself for all these years. It was like someone had lifted this huge weight off my shoulders that I had been carrying around for years...like breathing in a lungful of air after being underwater for too long...It was such a relief. [Tina]

Even if voluntary disclosure remains with one person only, the release of tension can be enormous for the self-injuring person, especially when it follows a previous policy of complete secrecy.

When self-injury is deliberately made known to others who do not self-injure, it is often done so to people whom the individual feels are trustworthy and who are expected to respond sympathetically (sympathetic others (Goffman, 1963:19)). Often these 'normals' (also referred to as the 'wise' by Goffman, 1963:28), who become 'privy' to the secret life of the self-injuring individual, are not family members, but close friends or professional counsellors in the voluntary sector. What sets these individuals apart in their relationship with the stigmatised individual is their contention that 'the individual with a fault need feel no shame nor exert self-control, knowing that in spite of his failing he will be seen as an ordinary other' (Goffman, 1963:28). Those individuals who are deemed trustworthy and who are expected to react in a non-judgemental and supportive fashion are those most likely to be confided in. Sally describes her experiences of this ethos being displayed by staff at a voluntary counselling organisation:

> Whenever I went for counselling to the rape crisis and sexual abuse centre, I had the permission to talk about my experiences of the abuse and all of the feelings and thoughts I had around that and the self-harm...I had the permission I suppose. I felt like I could talk about whatever I wanted...before I would have been waiting for the men in white coats to come and when they didn't it was good. I had the space to talk...no one judges you and says 'Oh that was a silly thing to do'. Nobody criticises you. [Sally]

Sally's account highlights the role played by the wise in two main areas. First, non-judgemental support can have a minimising effect on one's felt stigma. Second, the relaxed and non-threatening atmosphere facilitated in such therapeutic sessions promotes 'permission' and 'space' for periods of self-reflection and a greater understanding of one's position:

> They just accept that that's your way of coping...They listen to what it does for you...They help you work through why you cut...what it means to you and the whole process...Then you grow to understand it yourself.... [Sally]

Similar stages of self-recognition as this one in Sally's 'cutting career' were repeated by many participants and are not unlike the 'turning points' in Goffman's 'moral career'. He marked these as times

> ...when the individual was able to think through his problem, learn about himself, sort out his situation and arrive at a new understanding of what is important and worth seeking in life. (Goffman, 1963:40)

Self-injury, as we have discussed, is generally a secretive and solitary practice. Prior to the beginning of the new millennium especially, the isolation experienced by people who self-injured themselves was often intensified by a lack of awareness of the existence of other people like themselves. In fact many of this study's participants, like Nora who began her self-injury before the mid-1990s, believed that they had invented the behaviour:

> I really thought I was the only person ever to do this. It made me feel so different from everybody else...like I must be mad because I cut myself when I feel bad and having anyone find out about it was totally out of the question cus I thought I'd definitely get locked up or something. The when I realised there were other people who did it, it was like one of them 'eureka' moments. It makes you feel...I still was ashamed, but I suppose, I felt a bit more normal, if that's the right word. [Nora]

Knowledge of other people who also self-injure may be ascertained through various mediums and will be discussed in Chapter 8. Although someone who embarks on self-injury today is more likely than in previous generations to have heard about the behaviour prior to beginning it themselves, it is still common for the behaviour to be activated spontaneously and independent of such awareness. Levels of 'felt' stigma escalate under conditions of isolation and loneliness, so it would seem reasonable to assume that the reverse is also true. Whether or not actual acquaintances are made with other self-injuring people, the realisation that they exist, after self-injuring in psychological isolation, can have a diminishing effect on one's felt stigma. This brings us to another group of 'sympathetic others'. Aside from the 'wise', those who share the stigma can play a vital role in how the individual views him/herself in relation to his/her failing and the rest of society:

> Knowing from their own experience what it is like to have this particular stigma, some of them can provide the individual with instruction in the tricks of the trade and with a circle of lament to which he can withdraw for moral support and for the comfort of feeling at home, at ease, accepted as a person who is really like any other normal person. (Goffman, 1963:20)

Steve's relationship with a self-injuring friend, whom he met at a mental health day centre, is an example of a sympathetic other who shares the stigma. Not only does she act as a willing receptacle for Steve's 'sad tale accounting' (Goffman, 1963:21), she also provides practical first aid, in a more sympathetic fashion than Steve had come to expect, on visits to accident and emergency departments:

STEVE: When I come in here, my friend Paula, who also self-harms, knows me so well and knows when I've been cutting. She'd ask if I'm OK. I know when she's been self-harming too…

THERESA: Does it help having Paula…you know having a friend who also cuts and who understands?

STEVE: Yea very much so.… We don't talk about it in depth, like I've just done with you. You know, the exact details…. But apart from that, they're more like feelings and stuff and knowing that she knows how I feel…. We know how each other feels and about the uneasiness and knowing if you're going to do it. She'd patch me up too…. I wouldn't go to the hospital for help. Because any time you go there you're treated like a leper…you know?…. You've done that to yourself…. Made to wait ages for treatment and man-handled…. You know your wounds are scrubbed, not dabbed gently…You were just a waste of time. [Steve]

It is also interesting to note here, in relation to the bond that can develop between the stigmatised, a certain satirical connection from which non-self-injuring individuals are usually excluded:

> We [Steve and his self-injuring friend, Paula] have a bit of a dark sense of humour about it. When Gillette bring out a new blade, I'd love to get her a tee-shirt with it on the front. That's how we laugh about it between us. But if someone else tried that sense of humour we'd be really offended... you know? [Steve]

This exclusive in-group of camaraderie, created solely for the stigmatised, and, on occasion, exceptional 'sympathetic others' is reminiscent of Goffman's (1963:29) referral to the changed 'utilisation' of the word 'Nigger', between African Americans amongst themselves, from a term of derision to one expressing collective pride in a shared identity. Similar terminology, or humour attempted by non-members of the select group, would be interpreted of course, as Steve commented, as highly offensive. Steve and Paula's relationship is an example of association between two people on the basis of their shared stigma. Such affiliations, where they exist however, do not necessarily have to interact on a face-to-face level. As we will discuss in Chapter 8, it is increasingly possible to gain on virtual levels, such as those formed via the World Wide Web, a similar sense of connection with others who self-injure.

Redefinition

Drinkers drink, eaters eat and cutters cut

Chapter 4 of this book introduced the concept of the trajectory of suffering as proposed by Riemann and Schütze (2005) and its relevance to people who self-injure. Following on from the discussion on the main throes of the trajectory, it is possible to follow the path as it continues through stages during which opportunities to control and escape one's suffering are opened. In the course of off-peak periods in the trajectory, chances for reflection can promote a favourable environment in which to redefine one's suffering in a pain limiting way. Steve, Ella and Jane, whose experiences illustrated earlier discussions, had moved away from the original sources of their suffering (in a physical sense at least), and had begun periods of reflection on their life circumstances and their relationship with self-injury.

Simultaneously, they had begun to gain more control over their self-injury, which was often followed by the development of techniques aimed at maximising self-injury functions, even leading to ritualisation. As one's self-injury, as presented in this book, is interlocked with suffering, an interpretation of one's relationship with both elements is required. Aoife refers to an ancient Chinese proverb to express how she was able to achieve a degree of control over painful memories and subsequent use of self-injury:

> Well after a while I think I was able to see things in a different way. I know now that I cut myself to cope with being abused by the neighbour when I was too young to stop him and had no one to help me. I suppose it's like that saying 'know yourself and your enemy and you will win a hundred battles'. It kind of helps knowing why you do it, you know, the reasons behind it, because for me that was the first step towards taking control. (Tina)

Steve, at the time of interview was regularly self-injuring in a highly ritualised manner. His interpretation of his situation was unambiguous: Self-injury had emerged from and continued as a means to cope with extreme suffering. Steve's childhood was marred by severe physical, sexual and emotional abuse from his earliest memories before the age of five years and from a number of perpetrators whom Steve relied upon as caregivers. While he revealed traumatic experiences in all these areas, he summed up his reasons for self-injury as long-term rejection:

> When I see him [his father] I just feel rejection and that just sums up my whole life ... Rejection, Rejection, Rejection ... I've been rejected my whole life ... Rejected by my mother and my father, rejected in the homes [statutory, institutional childcare settings], in relationships, my marriage ... just rejection the whole way ... That's the one way I would describe why I self-harm ... rejection. [Steve]

Although he displayed clarity in his perception of the situation and a great deal of control over his self-injury in as far as ritualistic elements were concerned, Steve had been unsuccessful up to this point in constructing an account of his circumstances which would open prospects for a move away from self-injury as a way of coping.

Chapter 6 introduced the concept of accounting, as proposed by Goffman (1963), to illustrate how stigmatised individuals present plausible stories to non-stigmatised others in order to minimise negative reactions. They may, for example, invent narratives of scratching cats to explain tell-tale signs of stigma in a more socially acceptable manner. This technique is drawn upon extensively not only in relation to stigma, but additionally to ease suffering in other areas. Accounting to others and to oneself is a highly effective strategy for redefining and resisting stigma and repackaging negative experiences into more palatable interpretations. The Thomas theorem states that '…if men define situations as real, they are real in their consequences' (Thomas 1928, as cited in Merton, 1995:380). In the context of people who self-injure, choosing to define one's experiences (or elements of it) as less painful may translate into a reduction in one's suffering. It should be noted that this statement is not intended to invalidate or undermine the intensity of undergone trauma. Rather, it refers to a technique employed by some people who self-injure to reduce suffering where possible.

At the time of speaking to me, Ella had not self-injured for a number of months. During our conversation she revealed an account which had helped her come to terms with and lessen the intensity of some distressing childhood memories. On reflecting upon the roles played by her parents in her suffering, loathing for her sexually abusive father was evident: 'He's dead now, thank God'. Her relationship with the memory of her mother, however, was not so clear-cut. She loved her mother, but as a child was deeply confused and hurt that she failed to protect her from long-term sexual abuse. It was not until she had reached this stage in the trajectory that Ella was able to construct an account of her mother's position which allowed her to forgive the failure or inability to end abuse:

> I idolised my mummy, but at the time when I told her [that she was being sexually abused by her father], I was disgusted at her, cus if it had been me…I know this sounds dramatic, but if I was her, I would have had him arrested…put in jail…or I would have knifed the bastard…But in them days it was completely different…cus she had 12 kids and she had to rear them herself. [Ella]

Ella considered the hardship her mother would potentially have had to endure if she had taken action against her husband, Ella's father, to expose him as a paedophile and have him removed from the family home. She had previously mentioned that her father was physically abusive to everyone in the household including her mother. After many periods of reflection, Ella's perception of her mother's lack of action on her behalf changed. She sympathised with her mother's difficult circumstances. Threats of violence alongside other factors such as potential financial difficulties meant that Ella's mother would have had to face life as a single parent with twelve children to look after, and perhaps more significantly, the shame the family would suffer if people in her community were to discover the reason why her (highly respected) husband had left the family home. Ella did not underestimate the seriousness and extent of the suffering endured in her life. She was, however, able to redefine one painful memory, in as far as her mother's betrayal was concerned, to one in which she chose to remember events with understanding and empathy. Accounting to herself in this way promoted a reduction in her own suffering.

Jane was also not self-injuring at the time of interview and had not done so for over a year. She recalled her childhood as being a highly controlled and invalidating environment and directly linked forced suppression of negative emotions to subsequent self-injury. After many periods of reflection, Jane managed to cast a new and more positive light on memories of a domineering and oppressive mother which allowed her to minimise her mother's responsibility in her suffering:

> It was strange... I had a difficult relationship with my mother. We weren't very close. She found it really difficult to communicate towards me... It wasn't her fault. That was just the way she was. She was brought up that way. But it was instilled in me at home that I wasn't allowed to be angry, or sad... and um... or cross... and everything was turned in on me. My mum said 'don't you talk about anything to do with this family with anyone'. Maybe she just didn't realise the effect it was having on me and if she did she might have been different. [Jane]

Although Jane mitigated her mother's role in her troubled upbringing, her interpretation of damaging repercussions was nonetheless clear: Her childhood environment had led her to self-injure:

> When I was growing up I had to keep everything inside me. And it came out through cutting. And when I was 17, even though it was triggered by my boyfriend at the time, I found that it was a great relief, because it was the only way I could get out what was inside me. I can't talk to anyone but I can get it out this way. When I started cutting there was no pain. It was what it meant for me. It was the fact that this was something that I was in control of. Nobody knew about it at that stage. I did it when I wanted to and nobody else could tell me not to. The most important reason I did it was for the relief of pressure that I got. Um...I didn't know how to release it any other way. [Jane]

The conglomeration of disclosure to the right audience, sympathetic feedback, periods of reflection, redefinition of one's suffering and the like is generally accompanied by boosts in self-esteem and simultaneous reductions in felt stigma. It is often at this point that people are ready to reject stigma, both in terms of self-injury and possibly also related stigmas, such as those of sexual abuse. The transformation in Sally's opinion of herself and her self-injury, for example, is clear:

> I spent from I was eight years old thinking I was a freak...thinking I was bad...thinking I was dirty...feeling ashamed about who I was...what I was...what was happening to me...Do you know what?...I'm not a freak. Just because I cut I'm not a freak...I cut...I cope. [Sally]

Anne, like Sally, also refuses to feel ashamed of her self-injury. In fact she views it as having had a positive effect on her life:

> I wouldn't look at it negatively. Self-injury was not one of the bad things in my life. It was one of the good things. I don't regret that I did it and I wouldn't judge anyone else for doing it. [Anne]

Techniques to redefine self-injury and reject stigma are evident, especially when felt stigma is at a low ebb and energy to resist it begins to increase. Often the first of these strategies involves reclassification of the behaviour as more acceptable. A useful concept is Pfuhl's application of the term 'normalisation' to describe how the stigmatised individual 'seeks to render normal and morally acceptable that which has heretofore been regarded as abnormal and immoral' (Pfuhl, 1986:163). Sally gives an example of normalisation in her comparison of self-injury with other, more socially acceptable forms of self-harm:

> Maybe it's not a positive way to cope but is it positive to eat yourself silly? Or is it positive to drink yourself silly?...Yea you get people boasting about getting drunk...You know 'I got absolutely smashed last night'. But nobody says 'Yea, I cut the arms off myself last night'...I wouldn't advocate it [self-injury] as a way to cope in the same way I wouldn't tell you 'Get a bottle of vodka down your neck and you'll feel better'. It's hard for people to understand that drinkers drink, eaters eat and cutters cut. [Sally]

However, whereas Herman uses the term normalisation to describe how stigmatised individuals 'deny that their behaviour or attribute is deviant' (Herman, 1993:310), many people who self-injure continue to perceive self-injury as a deviant behaviour. It is in their comparison of the behaviour to more socially tolerated forms of self-harm, such as alcohol abuse, or over/under eating that they present self-injury as what Goffman (1963:130) refers to, as a 'normal deviance'. 'Of course it's wrong to cut yourself, but no more wrong than stuff that other people do' [Tina].

Related to this technique is a strategy used to 'condemn the condemners' (Sykes and Matza, 1957). Again the individual accepts the deviant label, but plays down its significance in comparison to more serious behaviours of those who would condemn self-injury. The technique of normalisation strives to elevate self-injury to the status of socially acceptable deviancy. In contrast, condemnation of the condemners is aimed mainly at challenging the hypocrisy of those 'normals' who would stigmatise people who self-injure, while their own worse behaviour goes unchallenged. Tina's example illustrates this point:

> There's far worse things than cutting yourself to release the unbearable feelings that you have inside you. I don't drink, I don't

smoke, I don't do drugs. My self-injury is enough. My kids are well looked after. They know nothing about my self-injury. I've done well to hide it from them…it wouldn't be fair on them if they found out. They would be distraught if they knew. I mean at least I don't harm anyone else…my ex would have gone out and got pissed [alcohol intoxicated] then came home and beat anyone that got in his way. Yet he would have been the first to condemn me if he'd have known about my cutting. [Tina]

In a similar vein to that of the economist, some people who self-injure will also carry out a cost/benefit analysis of their actions. Self-injury becomes, for many, the best course of action from a number of less appealing and less rewarding choices. Many participants in this study reported a psychological weighing up of the benefits gained by the use of self-injury against personal and social costs incurred by the action. The main benefit reported was self-injury as suicide prevention, as Sally explains:

It was damage limitation…it stopped me from killing myself. If I didn't do it I would not be here…I would be dead. So as far as I'm concerned I had no choice really. [Sally]

Similarly for Eve, self-injury was a premeditated alternative to a deliberate drug overdose:

I remember thinking 'It's a toss up between an overdose here or just getting rid of this anxiety'…. um…and I decided then…I did make a conscious decision to cut myself. Taking an overdose could have killed me but in cutting myself, I was in control. Both ways would have ended the mental pain I was in, but cutting was more reliable and safer in my opinion. So that's what I did. [Eve]

Even though everyone I spoke to was aware of the high social and personal costs of self-injury, many made a deliberate decision to carry on cutting or burning themselves. Tina, for example, weighed up costs, in terms of stigma, against the benefits she knew would be forthcoming from self-injury:

You know that you shouldn't be doing it, you know…covering yourself with scars…and you know what you'll have to face if people find out about it…you know they'll treat you like a freak…stuff like that…But at the end of the day, it's like…It's just a few wee cuts and then you can carry on with life…doing stuff you need to do…looking after the kids and functioning with your daily life. I wish I didn't hurt myself, but…put it this way, if I didn't, I don't know how I'd get by. [Tina]

At this stage in the 'cutting career' [Sally] we can see an element of self-determination and decisiveness in the behaviour. Two people who spoke to me went as far as to uphold the behaviour as their prerogative. Could we go further and say that self-injury is a lifestyle choice for some? The concept of self-injury as the independent and autonomous choice of the individual has been rejected, in the main, by feminist scholars. From this point of view, those who self-injure are traumatised by their suffering and are not conscious of the underlying dynamics compelling their actions (Liebling et al., 1997). Claims made by some people who self-injure, that the behaviour is deliberately and freely chosen, would be rejected in the feminist ideology as a form of false consciousness, under which they are incapable of viewing their actions as being influenced and conditioned by wider social structures (Jeffreys, 2000; Strong, 1998). Adler and Adler's position on the feminist standpoint is that it overlooks or rejects 'the ascription of agency to politically incorrect behaviour' (Adler and Adler, 2007:561). The position taken in this book, based on the experiences of people who self-injure, lies somewhere in the middle of the argument: Self-injury can begin as a response to psychological suffering over which there is little control, particularly at the outset. Levels of control can increase, however, as the trajectory of suffering progresses and chances for self-determination are opened. When they speak about independent choice in whether to self-injure or not, people are often likely to be referring to decisions made from the limited range of options they feel is, or was, open to them. For the majority, refusing to accept stigma, comparing self-injury to other ways of coping and advances in one's self-governance fall short of advocating or claiming self-injury as a lifestyle choice. It is more often the case when discussing choices available regarding self-injury that regret and sadness is expressed in relation to the original source of suffering, but for which self-injury would likely not have begun. Sam illustrates this point:

I'm just making the best out of a bad situation. I know all the reasons why not to cut myself, but I didn't have any say over stuff that happened. When my uncle was abusing me, I couldn't stop it. I didn't understand it. I couldn't tell anyone. I didn't have control. I don't think anything in particular ever gave me the idea to start biting my tongue. I just started doing that and then after a while it moved on to cutting...but it worked and I felt in control of the terrible pain inside me. And the way I look at it now, I'm taking control the best I can. [Sam]

Successful employment of stigma management strategies may also prompt individuals to broaden their personal battle with stigma management to a wider societal front. Perhaps the optimal tactic in the war on one's own stigma is to become politically active in reducing that stigma in other people and in the eyes of the general public. It could be argued that all the people who spoke to me were politically active, given the fact that they took part in this research. Most of them expressed a desire to raise awareness of self-injury from the perspective of those who practise it. They hoped that speaking out might improve how people who self-injure are viewed and treated by others. An additional objective behind their political activism was to directly 'help' others who were struggling with the behaviour and related issues. Mike, for example, gave newspaper and television interviews about his self-injury and sexual abuse. One of the reasons he gave for sharing private experiences in public was his wish to dispel some of the myths that he felt had grown up around self-injury:

It was difficult to speak out about what happened to me. But I felt I had to. People need to know about this type of thing. Secrecy just makes matters worse. When people see someone with the signs of self-injury on them, they jump to conclusions...that they must be trying to kill themselves. Or if it's not suicide then it's attention seeking or an attempt to manipulate someone. And when someone has never self-injured then it's hard for them to understand. You can't blame them for just taking on what society tells them about it. [Mike]

Steve's experience of humiliating and disparaging treatment at the hands of medical staff has been documented in this book. The desire to improve treatment for people who seek medical attention in relation to their self-injury was his motivation behind taking part in research:

> I know what it's like to be made to feel like a piece of shit. You're already feeling bad and they [medical personnel] make you worse. Doctors and nurses need a better understanding of what it's like to self-injure. We don't all do it just to waste their time. If I can stop one person from getting stitched up without anaesthetic, or treated like a time waster then I'm happy. [Steve]

Sally was particularly active politically. She attended and participated at conferences where she spoke about her experiences of self-injury and sexual abuse. In addition, she gave media interviews, took part in research and wrote poetry. Like Steve, Sally had suffered negative reactions from others regarding her self-injury and wanted to improve how self-injuring individuals are portrayed in society. She was especially motivated to reach out in solidarity to other people who self-injure to ease suffering and isolation:

> I feel strongly about it. I felt for years that it was me who was at fault, but I know now that I was just surviving using the only coping strategy I had. When you're in the middle of it, it's so lonely. And feeling so lonely makes everything else worse, cus you think you're the only one and you feel bad and terribly guilty. I want to help people who self-injure because I know what they are going through. There is light at the end of the tunnel. I understand it better now myself and want to help others get through without feeling so alone and ashamed. [Sally]

Political activism is not entirely altruistically driven for the support of other similarly stigmatised individuals or to educate the general public in a more positive image of people with the stigma. To fall short of what society deems 'norms' of behaviour, for whatever reason, can devastate one's self-image. Political activism can offer a path away from this position.

> Taking part in research like this makes me feel useful…like I'm doing something positive with myself. It makes me feel better

about me to know that I'm helping other people who self-injure. If I can help people who cut themselves like I do, by talking about my self-injury, then they mightn't feel so alone. And also, if other people like their family and friends read this then they might understand it better too. So it can only be good for everyone to talk about it and understand it…and that makes me feel good because I've done a good turn. [Tina]

The adoption of a new and positive raison d'être after periods marked by negativity and poor sense of worth can significantly contribute to the promotion of one's self-confidence. Herman (1993) identified in her work on stigma management strategies of ex-psychiatric patients how some individuals applied similar strategies to those discussed above, not only in their personal lives, but on public fronts also. She isolated three functions served by political activism which are equally relevant to self-injury:

> (a) it repudiated standards of normalcy (standards to which they could not measure up) and the deviant labels placed on these individuals; (b) it provided them with a new, positive non-deviant identity, enhanced their self-respect, and afforded ex-patients a new sense of purpose; and (c) it served to propagate this new positive image of ex-mental patients to individuals, groups, and organisations in society. The payoff from political activism was, then, both personal as well as social. (Herman, 1993:306)

Listening to people's experiences and picking out common themes makes it possible to chart how control can be gained in one's state of affairs. The episodes of losing one's self-orientation during peak 'trajectory' crises, self-injury and the employment of makeshift strategies to avoid or minimise stigma can give way to periods of reflection and a workable perception of one's situation. Opportunities to reflect on the experience of living through a trajectory of suffering, with or without the assistance of significant others, opens up possibilities to 'work upon' or 'escape' the trajectory (Riemann and Schütze, 2005:132). Channelling effort into a positive redefinition of one's affairs and helping others to do the same can greatly improve one's self-esteem. The process does not necessarily progress in one direction only. Setbacks can be expected in what Aoife analogises as a 'two steps forward, one step back' procedure. It is possible, however, to make significant gains in the direction of a new, more optimistic self-perception:

> I'm not the person I was two years ago. Back then I was confused and didn't control anything in my life. Don't get me wrong, I still have days when I feel like I can't face the world but I suppose a lot of people are like that. In general though, I'm definitely more settled, more confident and more in control than I was. I have a new and more positive way of looking at things. I had a hard time when I was young, things happened that shouldn't have, I self-injured to cope and today I'm a stronger person than I was. I don't feel ashamed anymore and that in itself is so liberating. [Aoife]

Resilience

> *It just sort of came to a natural stop. I used to cut almost every other day…Now I don't any more.*

Everyone who took part in this study had suffered negative experiences. They all revealed emotionally invalidating childhood environments and over half of them disclosed sexual and physical abuse additionally. Emotional invalidation can lead to psychological distress and suppression of negative emotions, as can sexual abuse and associated stigma. Many people, at times, try to alter their feelings. However, it is practically impossible to stifle one's emotions indefinitely and attempting to do so can result in further problems. Tina's 'elephant' analogy usefully illustrates how attempts to suppress, or simply push out, negative thoughts and feelings can become a vicious cycle, in which unwanted emotions are aggravated and increased in their intensity:

> A feeling is a feeling. There's no getting away from that. I've tried shutting off my emotions, but it's impossible. You can't just make yourself stop thinking about stuff and feeling a certain way. If only it was as easy as that. You can't push them out of your head either. I try to think of it like…I mean if someone says to you 'Don't think of an elephant', what's the first thing you think about?…An elephant. And the more you try not to think about

the elephant, the more the trying not to think about it, makes you think about it [laughs] ... Do you know what I mean? It's the same for bad thoughts and feelings. You can't just shut them off and you can't push them away and the more you try, the worse they get. [Tina]

For people who self-injure, attempting to suppress distressing thoughts and feelings is usually the first line of attack in the struggle to regulate emotion. Some people will then turn to alcohol and/or drugs to keep emotions in check. Self-injury is an extreme but effective short-term solution to the problem of releasing and controlling unwanted emotion. These and other damaging activities can be used alternately or in conjunction with each other.

About a third of the people who spoke to me were, at the time of interview, no longer self-injuring. In this group, few could say with certainty that they would never self-injure again. It was more often the case that, although they had reached a period of months or years marked by no self-injury, they fell short of guaranteeing permanent discontinuance.

Often the first step away from self-injury is to cease attempts to change or remove negative emotions. Acceptance of one's unwanted feelings is not the same as surrendering to them in the resignation that one will always suffer from them. It is about acknowledging that they are there and that they are temporary. In the beginning, it is often difficult to let go of what can be overwhelming urges to resist negative feelings, but many people who have moved away from self-injury learn this technique. Mike found a supportive counsellor who assisted him in coming to terms with sexual abuse and self-injury. He found that once he was able to stop struggling with his distressing thoughts and feelings, they lost their intensity:

He [counsellor] helped me accept my past ... and the best part about the past, is that it's in the past. It took a lot of time and practice and talking to him about it. But then after a while, I stopped fighting the memories and the guilt and the hurt. And I knew I was finally on the road to recovery. It didn't mean that I was giving in to bad feelings. I was just accepting that they were there and if I let them just be there then after time they might lose their power over me. [Mike]

Some people who had managed to stop their self-injury reported a recognition that painful events in the past could not be changed and that the most constructive way of coping begins with acceptance. Future harm, however, could be averted or limited. Sam, for example, who had suffered sexual, physical and emotional abuse in childhood, avoided reminders of suffering as one of his main self-injury prevention tactics. At the time of interview, Sam had not self-injured for nearly two years and was particularly vocal about strategies he found helpful. One of these techniques involved limiting contact with members of his family of origin, whom he felt were detrimental to his psychological wellbeing:

> There's a lot of blame passed about in my family … a lot of damage was done when we were kids and thirty odd years later, there's still a lot of in-fighting going on. When I'm with my sisters now, it always ends up getting brought into the conversation and I feel all the old feelings starting up inside me. I've tried telling them that I don't want to talk about the old stuff and try changing the subject and stuff. But they don't listen. It's happened so many times now, when I thought I was doing well with my life and then all the shit is stirred up again and I take a nosedive straight into self-harm. I start biting my tongue and cutting myself and a whole cycle of shit starts. It's unfortunate, but I've learned a lot about myself over the years and I now know that I have to withdraw from people who just aren't good for the state of my mental health. [Sam]

Sympathetic others can be an invaluable resource for people in their attempts to move away from self-injury. Rachel (a 26-year-old, married office clerk who was rejected by her father in childhood) was helped by her husband and mother through occasions when she felt like self-injuring.

> You can't spend the rest of your life going to the kitchen for a knife when you can't cope? When I'm upset now, I will say to [husband] that I need time to myself. I talk to my mum sometimes. She always knows when I'm upset … and my husband listens to what's bothering me and tries to suggest things to cheer me up like go out with my friends …. [Rachel]

Similarly, Sam named an understanding spouse as his main source of support. According to Sam, his wife had helped him to raise his self-confidence considerably and had aided him in his acceptance of negative feelings when they started, in the assurance that, with patience, they would pass:

> My wife is just the best. I don't know what I would do without her. Sometimes I get these intrusive thoughts in my head about stuff that happened in my past and I know that if I didn't have her to run them past they would build in my head until I end up cutting myself. She just has this way of helping me to rationalise how I feel...the shame of the abuse and stuff. She tells me that it wasn't my fault that it happened...I was only a child. She says 'Take a deep breath and let the feeling wash over you. Don't try to fight it, just let it come and relax into it'. She tells me she loves me and that I should feel proud of myself for achieving all that I have in my life. [Sam]

Caring for other people and attending to one's daily responsibilities can help to focus one's attention away from one's own problems. Sam's drive to take care of his family and provide for their practical, financial and emotional needs aided him in his struggle with his difficult past. He felt that having them to care for was a positive distraction and was another factor in creating an opening for recovery:

> I feel so blessed that I have Jenny and the kids. They are my reason to get up and go to work every day to do my best for them. I never want my kids to feel fear and loneliness like I did...and all the other things...They keep me on the straight and narrow and I live every day thankful that I have them to care for. I want to give them all the love and care that I didn't get. I have been given a chance to get better...to get over what happened and I'm grabbing it. [Sam]

'Stopping for others' was cited as a common motivation for moving away from self-injury. Moreover, reasons of 'not wanting to hurt' loved ones or fear of irreparable damage, even complete break-down being caused to relationships if self-injury continued, were cited often. As well as channelling one's attention into caring for children, spouses and work commitments, some people with pets found that having a living creature depend upon them for life was also conducive to a successful move away from self-injury. John went so far as to credit his obligation to a pet cat as a suicide deterrent:

> I had a cat...a wee scrawny cat...if I hadn't have had that cat I know I would have been dead a long time ago...if I hadn't had responsibility for this life. Something to hang on for.... [John]

Anne was sexually abused by a family friend in childhood and was bullied at school in relation to her sexuality. She began to self-injure at 14 years of age. Anne alternated between cutting herself with blades and burning herself with an iron to gain 'relief' and 'distraction' from the self-blame she felt for having been sexually abused by a trusted family friend. Within a couple of years her self-injury intensified and she began to additionally use it a way to 'punish' herself for bisexual urges. Anne was not self-injuring when she took part in this study, at the age of 19 years, and attributed processes of maturity as the main explanation for cessation:

> It just sort of came to a natural stop. I used to cut almost every other day if not more. And now I don't any more. That's because some of the things that were in my mind, or some of the problems that I had, aren't problems any more. They don't make me angry, or they don't make me sad, or they don't make me hate myself so much that I have to cut. I think that's the only way you can ever stop...is when things don't bother you as much. A lot of me stopping is down to maturity to see that certain things that happened...that I believed were my fault...I was abused...and when you're younger you just can't understand why things like that happen. You always have to blame someone and generally you blame yourself and then when you're older...well I just realised I'm not to blame. So I don't feel that I have to punish myself, or I don't get depressed as much about it, as I realised it's not my fault. I don't need to punish myself, cus I haven't done anything wrong. I just don't feel the need to do it as much now. [Anne]

As discussed in Chapter 2, most people who self-injure begin to do so in early adolescence, which implies that self-injury is associated with age-related issues affecting youth (Babiker and Arnold, 1997). As people grow from adolescence into young adulthood and beyond, their intellectual maturity too increases. As the developmental process continues, they may become more able to cast off some of the social conventions and norms of behaviour which curtailed their thoughts and actions to a greater degree than when they were younger (Babiker and Arnold, 1997).

Sally, Dawn and Jane wrote poetry about their experiences of self-injury and associated issues. Much of their poetry was written in adolescence, when their self-injury began and was at its height. Expressing one's thoughts and feelings in written forms of poetry, other forms of creative writing and diaries is a way to communicate and release tension. Moreover, poetry allows secretive or shameful phenomena, which might otherwise have to remain hidden due to social constraints, to be aired:

> There is much about the human condition...that can be revealed safely because it is 'disguised as a poem', giving voice to those silenced from within by self-doubt and from without by ostracism and prejudice. (Johnson and Chernoff, 2002:141)

Jane's poetry began as a response to her self-injury and suffering and, since then, she believes it has helped her to communicate without the restrictions that beset her in other areas of her life. She uses her poetry now as a positive way to channel and express emotions:

> Now my priorities have shifted a bit I have other things to focus on. The need to cut myself is much less but I feel it has the potential to be there if things go wrong again. I write poetry. It started in my mid teens. Um...it was directly related to self-harm and I wrote about my experiences of self-harm...What it meant to me...How it felt for me...Um...How I felt inside my head. But now my writing has evolved much more, um...its proper poetry now and I'm not writing about self-harm or depression...Um when I'm writing I feel more human...I couldn't survive without my writing. It is also like a substitute in a way, because it helps me focus how I'm feeling because I think about it when I'm writing...Um...Up until recently I was very guarded in what I wrote. Now I feel more able to freely express how I feel. [Jane]

One of the most successful methods of distraction and regulation of one's emotions mentioned by people, who manage to move away from self-injury, is exercise. In whatever form it takes – walking, running, swimming, cycling, gym or sport – exercise can offer enormous positive, physical and psychological benefits. Aoife cites yoga classes as invaluable in helping her to relax and diffuse negative feelings of stress without harming herself:

> I never would have thought it could have helped me until a friend dragged me along with her to a class one time. I really got into it and it's amazing, the calming effect it can have over you. I found it really helpful. It can be really physical. I mean you be out of breath at times doing it. There's also meditation and relaxation. So it's good for both body and mind. Sometimes now when I feel bad, I go up to my bedroom and do some yoga. It doesn't take long, after ten or 15 minutes I feel much better. The way you have to breath in yoga makes your body relax and slows down your racing heart. It helps you clear your mind and refocus your energy ... [Laughs] I suppose it's kinda like a drug in that sense ... but a really healthy one. [Aoife]

Psychological and physical wellbeing are interrelated. Physical exercise reportedly stimulates chemicals in the brain ('happy hormones') which elevate mood. People who take regular exercise find that all areas of life are enhanced. They look and feel better physically. They can feel happier and less stressed. Their self-confidence and self-worth are boosted. Their sleep is more restful. Their enjoyment of food is greater and they are more likely to eat a healthy diet. They may have a better social life and more fun in general (Royal College of Psychiatrists, 2009).

Physical activity does not have to be formal or take place in a sports centre. Others found that being more energetic in their general everyday activities aided the shift away from self-injury. Sam enjoys gardening and finds it beneficial in terms of exercise, distraction and for promoting relaxation in a positive way:

> As well as spending time with Jenny and the kids, I find gardening enjoyable. It can be physically demanding ... you know, you can get quite out of breath in the garden when you really throw

yourself into it. But I also find it relaxing after working hard all day. I work in sales, which is quite stressful. So it feels great to get home and to spend an hour or so outside, tending to some garden project or another. I sleep better and everything. I always found the evening time was the worse time of day for my self-harm. So I try to keep myself busy with something physical after dinner in the early evening and then I'm too busy to think about depressing stuff…and too tired…but a positive kind of tired. [Sam]

Rachel also recognised the importance of keeping busy in order to distract herself from unwanted emotions which, in the past, led to self-injury. Occupying oneself in order to take one's mind off negative emotions can be tiring when done over long periods. Rachel alternated between techniques of keeping busy with activities and relaxation with music:

I know now that if I don't get up and do something I will get worse. So I'll go out for a walk or go and see friends or something…I try to keep busy when I start to feel bad. But you can't keep busy all the time and sometimes it's trouble trying to relax that can stress me out. When I want to relax but can't, it just stresses me more. I love music…I listen to it from morning to night…and I'll lie on the bed and listen to my Ipod…and just lie until my eyes closed until I calm down…I find that if I put on relaxing music it can help. [Rachel]

It must be stated at this point that many of the above, as well as other tactics, may yet be out of reach, in terms of helpfulness for people who are in the main throes of a trajectory of suffering. Dawn recalled being offered, at the height of her suffering and cutting, psychiatric advice for techniques of self-injury avoidance:

He [psychiatrist] would give me methods for stopping, like putting elastic bands around your wrist and twanging them…Which I thought…was laughable. He was a really nice person, but it just didn't help. He might as well have tied the elastic band around a steam train and expected it to stop the train from hurtling off down the track. [Dawn]

This particular strategy was suggested to many people who had made themselves known to psychiatric professionals in relation to their self-injury, and is based on the assumption that a mild dose of pain delivered by snapping elastic on the wrist should negate the desire to do further damage. Most, like Dawn, who were in the depths of their suffering when this suggestion was presented to them, likened the rubber band method to a drop in the ocean in terms of helpfulness. Self-injury is a complex phenomenon. The dynamics which make cessation of self-injury possible are interrelated. The effectiveness of avoidance and distraction strategies can be limited when used in isolation. They can, however, be extremely helpful when employed as part of a holistic approach which includes acceptance of negative emotions and other factors discussed. Even when successful, there can still be periods of relapse into self-injury and other negative emotion regulation strategies. However, as testimonies in this book have shown, it is possible to move away from self-injury and lead a fulfilling and happy life.

8
Self-injury, Popular Culture and the Internet

[Untitled by Jane]

Who was it, brave enough to write
How 'one drags a blade through one's skin
Praying for the courage to press down'
Those are not my words
But I understand them

In Chapter 1, I introduced self-injury in a historical context, briefly charting its changing image in biblical, historical and medical realms. This final chapter will look in greater detail at the impact of recent sociological influences on the social face of self-injury. Mirroring the private appearance of self-injury is the public expression of the phenomenon. Awareness of self-injury is no longer as obscure as it once was. People who self-injure today are more likely than in previous decades to have knowledge of the behaviour before embarking on it themselves. In addition, knowledge of self-injury is no longer restricted to studies on individuals being psychiatrically treated (Adler and Adler, 2007, 2011). People who self-injure are much more diverse than presented previously. Structural shifts affecting how self-injury is viewed in society have been taking place over the past two decades or more. The first wave of these has been evident since the early 1990s when self-injury appeared in the popular culture and the second with the rise of the internet in the early 2000s.

Self-injury and popular culture

I was just watching TV ... Famous people were cutting themselves!

156

People who began to self-injure before the mid-1990s were more likely to have done so in unawareness of the behaviour in wider society. Mike, for example, who was in his forties when he spoke to me, began to spontaneously self-injure as an adolescent in the 1970s, believing that he 'was the only one in the world doing this'. Those participants who began their self-injury post mid-1990s, however, were more likely to have heard of the behaviour prior to beginning it. For example, Jane (aged 23 at the time of interview) 'got the idea off TV'. She began her self-injury aged 11 years in 1995 and recalled at that time watching a television programme in which self-injury was depicted as a way to relieve emotional distress associated with teenage angst. Her own self-injury began shortly after this exposure and rapidly developed on to a regular activity.

When those who began to self-injure in psychological isolation of other self-injuring people discovered that they were in fact not alone in self-injury they were often taken aback. Such discoveries were often stumbled across accidentally as the frequency with which self-injury was covered in the media increased. Tina began to cut herself in 1981 at the age of 15 years, without knowledge of other people who also did so. She describes the moment she learned she was not alone in self-injury and how her surprise was intensified in the discovery that a well-known public figure had shared her secret shame:

> I was just watching TV one evening and was flicking through the channels. I saw this programme…I can't remember the name of the show, but they were talking about people who hurt themselves and they were talking about Princess Diana who had spoken out about her self-harm. Well you could have knocked me down with a feather. I was totally gobsmacked. Other people…like famous people, were cutting themselves just like me. I've since learned about other famous people like Johnny Depp and Angelina Jolie…and I mean they all look so normal and they've done really well for themselves. You wouldn't think to look at them that they cut themselves to feel better, like me…Wow! [Tina]

Twenty years ago, revelations of self-injury by famous people were extremely unusual. Since then, however, according to Whitlock et al.

(2007:3), 'researchers speculate that its spread into popular culture gathered momentum in the 1990s when over 14 pop icons revealed self-injurious habits in various media outlets'. Some of the spheres of celebrity from which public disclosures have been made are the music and entertainment businesses, sport and royalty. American actor Johnny Depp revealed in a 1993 interview for a popular magazine that 'he always viewed his body as a journal and that the scars from the cutting [were] intense diary entries' (Johnstone, 2010:13). Since then, a long list of famous people have publicly admitted to self-injuring. One of the most well documented of these was made in the BBC Panorama interview with Princess Diana in 1995, in which she revealed to interviewer Martin Bashir how she had turned to self-injury and bulimia as coping strategies. In this extract she discusses her own meanings for the behaviour, misunderstandings among other people and how her experiences helped her in her role of advocate:

> DIANA: You have so much pain inside yourself that you try and hurt yourself on the outside … People see it as crying wolf or attention seeking. And they think because you're in the media all the time, you've got enough attention … So yes I did inflict upon myself, I didn't like myself. I was ashamed that I couldn't cope with the pressures.
>
> BASHIR: What did you actually do?
>
> DIANA: Well, I just hurt my arms and my legs and I work in environments now where I see women doing similar things and I'm able to understand completely where they're coming from. [BBC Panorama, 1995]

Actress Angelina Jolie uncovered details of her cutting and reasons for it in a biography: 'I went through a period when I felt trapped, cutting myself because I felt I was releasing something. It was honest' (Mercer, 2007:11). British athlete Kelly Holmes documented her self-injury in her autobiography. She self-injured in an attempt to deal with performance hindering injuries:

> [I] would break down again and get out the scissors to mark yet another day of injury. Once I even cut my chest – a cut that became very sore when I wore a crop top in the swimming pool that kept rubbing right over there. (Holmes, 2007:211)

Recently deceased, English singer-songwriter Amy Winehouse, famed for her mental health problems, substance misuse, volatile relationships and general self-destructive behaviour, was also known to self-injure. Her song 'Rehab', about her reluctance to seek professional help for problems with alcohol abuse is perhaps the most well-known in her discography. Winehouse publicly admitted to cutting the words 'I love Blake' into the skin on her abdomen (Gabrielle, 2011).

Celebrity disclosure of cutting and other forms of self-injury has caught the attention of the public and has been mirrored by the sharp rise in its portrayal in popular culture. Self-injury has been discussed in magazine and newspaper articles, chat shows and current affair programmes. British daytime current affair chat show 'The Wright Stuff' on Channel Five has documented self-injury (Youtube videos parts one and two, 2011). Similarly, television presenter Lorraine Kelly (ITV, 2007) has interviewed young people who self-injure regarding their experiences of self-injury and what it means to them. The behaviour has also captured American audiences, with numerous hosts such as Oprah Winfrey and Sally Jesse Raphael featuring self-injury and related topics on US daytime and primetime talk shows.

Self-injury has also appeared in film storylines. The film 'Girl interrupted' (2000), starring Winona Ryder, Brittany Murphy and Angelina Jolie, is an example of self-injury depiction as part of a movie plotline. Set in a mental institution, it displays self-injury wounds on the arm of one of the film's main actresses. 'Secretary' (2002) is a romantic comedy starring Maggie Gyllenhaal and James Spader. Although the plot centres on a submissive/dominant relationship between the leading actors, it also displays Gyllenhaal self-injuring by burning her thighs with a kettle.

Since its inception in 1995, British soap opera 'Hollyoaks' has been known to tackle the portrayal of contemporary and often controversial issues affecting society. It has been both praised and criticised for basing storylines on sensitive topics such as murder, child abuse, racism, homophobia, addiction and domestic violence. It was one of the first soap operas to include self-injury in a storyline. The plot follows a female character as she struggles with negative emotions and inwardly channels feelings of distress, disgust and hatred:

> Lisa's guilt and self-loathing led her straight to a high street chemist, where she found herself surrounded by everything she needed to satiate her urge to self-harm. (TV.Com, 2011)

Lisa subsequently self-injured in a bathroom by cutting herself.

The ITV 'Emmerdale' dramatisation of self-injury centres on character Holly Barton's struggle with drug addiction. While locked in her bedroom by her parents, in their desperate bid to detox her from drugs, she self-injures in an attempt to cope with the enforced 'cold turkey'. Holly is then discovered by her mother to have self-injured with a nail that had been used to attach wooden boards in front of the window to prevent her escape (Digital spy, 2011).

Self-injury also features on many American television productions. TV dramas such as 'Will and Grace', 'Grey's Anatomy' and '7th Heaven' (Nixon and Heath, 2009). Representations of self-injury and related matters can also be found in newspapers and magazines. Most of these articles are aimed at raising awareness and understanding of self-injury, especially for parents of young people whom they suspect or know are self-injuring:

> Often people that self harm will be embarrassed and ashamed of their problem and try to keep it a secret at all costs by hiding their scars under clothes or just pretending to be OK in public. It can be hard to know that anything is wrong and in this case, attention is probably the last thing they want. (Good to know Magazine, online version)

The last number of years has witnessed a deluge of books on the topic of self-injury. Many of these have been written by, and for, those in the medical and counselling professions and academics. Some are also intended for lay people including those who do and do not self-injure. Most focus on information/self-help and usually include examples of self-injuring case studies. They are often also illustrated with testimonies of people who self-injure. One of the most well-known and most referenced of these is the now classic *Bodies under siege: Self-mutilation and body modification in culture and psychiatry* by Armando Favazza (1996). This title was regarded as groundbreaking when first published in 1987 and is still considered by many as 'The Holy Grail' of self-injury books. There is also a smaller, non-medically orientated, group of books which have been emerging in more recent years. These tend to be autobiographical and/or fictional and focus more on experiences of people who self-injure. *Skin game* by Caroline Kettlewell (2000) is an example of an autobiographical account of self-injury. And from the fictional section *The luckiest girl in the world* by Steven Levenkron (1998) is about a young skater who struggles with self-destructive compulsions. Adler and Adler's (2011) book, 'The tender cut: Inside the hidden world of self-injury' represents the recent sociological interest in the behaviour. These authors draw upon their ten year longitudinal study involving interviews and online chat room postings to show how self-injury has 'spilled beyond psychiatric bounds' and 'into the broader reaches of the mainstream' (22). Self-injury is much more widespread than was previously realised and the demographic profile of people who self-injure, more diverse. They explore the social transformation of self-injury from narrow, medical definitions of recent decades to the broader, 21st century meaning.

Whatever the issue concerning society and the individual, reference will always be found in the lyrics of poem and song. Whether private, or public, troubled or joyous, the history of humanity can be charted in folk music passed down through generations in both written and oral forms. Today, even though there are multiple means of communication, music is still as popular a way to express one's thoughts as ever it was. References to self-injury can be found in many popular present-day song lyrics. Alternative rock band 'Manic Street Preachers' provide an example:

Roses in the hospital, try to pull my fingernails out...
Roses in the hospital, stub cigarettes out on my arm...
Forever delayed. The west scratches onto my skin. (Excerpt from 'Roses in the hospital', by Manic Street Preachers, online lyrics)

Similarly, Australian born singer-songwriter Sia Furler has implied self-injury in her compositions:

Help, I have done it again
I have been here many times before
Hurt myself again today
And, the worst part is there's no-one else to blame. (Excerpt from 'Breath me' by Sia, online lyrics)

In as far as representations of self-injury in popular culture are concerned it is difficult to find one area in which it has not penetrated over the past two decades. Public disclosures of self-injury by house-hold names, as well as representations in visual and auditory for-mats, have all raised awareness of the phenomenon, fed the public's interest and aspired more understanding of the behaviour to be forthcoming.

Self-injury and the internet

It's like everything on the internet, there's some great stuff and some real crap

Sam is an example of someone who self-injured for years in isolation before finding out that there are other people who are also using this way of coping:

> I always thought I was the only person who did this to themselves and for the reasons I do. But a couple of years ago I came across self-injury on the internet. I was really surprised and shocked that there were other people like me. The more I investigated the web-sites the more I realised that there were loads of people who do this to cope with stuff. [Sam]

The internet has flourished since the late 1990s. Children born since the dawn of the new millennium are the first generation to be raised from birth in a world of widespread internet accessibility. In the United Kingdom over 76 per cent of adults were accessing the internet in 2009 (ONS, 2009). This figure is rising as, accord-ing to internet usage statistics for 2010, the percentage rose to 82.5 per cent (Miniwatts Marketing Group, 2010). Similar statistics exist in the United States with percentages increasing when surveys are restricted to the young, as almost nine out of every ten American youth are logging on regularly (Lenhart et al., 2005). The internet is now often the first port of call for information on news, shop-ping, interests, health guidance, education and 'how to' advice. One can download music and films and take part in social networking all without having to move from the computer screen or handheld device, almost anywhere in the world. Today one would be extremely hard pressed to think of any sphere of life which cannot be found on the World Wide Web. There is now a rapidly growing number of websites offering an outlet for confidential interaction and support among self-injuring individuals (Adler and Adler, 2007, 2011). The entry of terms such as 'self-injury', 'self-harm', 'self-cutting', 'self-burning' into Google or Yahoo search engines on a computer results in literally millions of hits. Self-injury has exploded onto the internet much in the same way in which other stigmatised and covert behaviours such as anorexia have appeared in the past (Norris et al., 2006). In 2005, there were believed to be 400 self-injury websites (Whitlock et al., 2006b), increasing to 500 within a year (Whitlock et al., 2007). One of the main British sites is 'Firstsigns', a self-injury guidance and network support (available at www.firstsigns.org.uk). 'Firstsigns' is a voluntary online user-led organisation founded in 2002 to raise awareness of self-injury and also provide information and support for anyone affected by it. A forum for discussion is provided and links to social networking websites (discussed below) maximise the organisation's awareness raising potential. Members can also avail of newsletters, seminars, workshops and events such as the annual National Self-injury Awareness Day (SIAD) and various 'get together' meetings throughout the United Kingdom. In addition, they supply wrist bracelets and keyrings to raise awareness of self-injury and reduce stigma. Most self-injury websites encourage discussions on behaviour and related issues. Sharing of experiences, questions, replies, debates and so on, largely take place via message boards which are generally arbitrated by the website moderators. In order to post a message or take part in a discussion, members usually have to go through a process of registration in which they must agree to adhere to board policies (or 'house rules') regarding use of offensive language and discussions which are seen to deliberately promote acts of self-injury. In addition, posts which contain graphic descriptions of self-injury acts and associated emotions are often labelled as 'Triggering'. It is considered that the reading of such posts could have negative consequences for some readers, promoting feelings which could potentially lead to episodes of self-injury. Although warnings are given and moderators endeavour to maintain websites as 'safe' spaces in which to explore self-injury and related issues, the decision to read potential self-injury causative posts and other material is ultimately left to individuals.

The internet is constantly evolving. Recent innovations have created a virtual world for people in which they can search out and interact with others, and socially taboo subjects such as self-injury can be freely discussed without fear of consequence for the individual who logs on. There are many websites on which such interaction is possible. YouTube (available at www.youtube.com), for example, is a video sharing website which since its creation in 2005 has allowed users to upload, share and comment on videos. Individuals can upload to such YouTube, video representations of their experiences and meanings of self-injury which can then be viewed within seconds by a worldwide audience. Often the videos are set to music and viewers can comment on the videos and comments posted by other registered members. Exchanges can be heated and language unrestricted. Entry of the terms 'self-injury' and 'self harm' into the YouTube search bar produced 12,300 and 13,700 'hits' respectively, for videos containing these words in their description. Although some of the video descriptors use both these (and others, e.g. 'self-mutilation' or 'cutting') terms interchangeably in each video, it gives an idea of the amount of interest in the desire to both post and view information, opinions and experiences about the behaviour. Videos are usually short (most often between 2 and 10 minutes). Most are posted by people who want to communicate their own self-injury experiences with others. Others are created by professionals, in which advice and information is offered for people who self-injure, their families, friends, other professionals and anyone else who is generally interested in finding out about the behaviour.

As well as websites for specific self-injury interests and video sharing, the topic of self-injury has also infiltrated general social networking websites which have sprung up since the mid-2000s. Some examples of these are 'MySpace' (available at www.myspace.com), 'Bebo' (available at www.bebo.com) and 'Facebook '(available at www.facebook.com). 'Facebook' is currently the largest social networking service website on the internet. Since its launch in 2004, Facebook usage has spread rapidly worldwide and membership has reputedly reached 600 million active users (Carlson, 2011). An award winning feature film about its creation has been highly successful (The Social Network, 2011). Facebook and similar websites allow users to create and update their personal profiles, keep in touch with friends, interact with strangers, share photos, music, videos and games and join additional networks created and managed by themselves or other organisations. Like many of the self-

injury user websites, social networking and video sharing websites
are also regulated and members are warned that uploading offensive material can result in removal of items and the possible closure
of offending members' accounts. However, in reality, such websites
usually rely on users to report antisocial material which, even when
flagged, can remain in the public domain for long periods of time
until a member of website staff decides to remove it. Further, barred
users can simply open a fresh account under a new user name and
identification. Of the internet social networking users who spoke to
me about their self-injury, many commented that they had viewed
detailed photographs of self-injury and videos demonstrating acts
of self-injury including graphic close-up shots of people cutting
their skin with blades. Sam describes his experience of viewing disturbing pictures of self-injury and his viewpoint on the usefulness
of the internet in general:

> The internet is fantastic, but you do have to be careful. If you're at
> all vulnerable and you come across some upsetting pics or com-
> ments, it could set you back. Self-injury is all over the internet.
> Some of the stuff is really good and really helpful ... you know peo-
> ple wanting to share their stories and help others who hurt them-
> selves like this. It's not always about the actual cutting and stuff.
> It's more important to be able to share how you feel about things,
> than focusing on the actual self harm. But I mean, yea, I've come
> across some really graphic stuff, showing up-close pictures of bad
> injuries, blood and flesh and it's not pretty. I don't see the point of
> that at all. All it is, is upsetting and it doesn't get to the core issue
> at all. Then of course you have people who know fuck all about it
> coming on and making really hurtful remarks about it ... calling
> them freaks and telling them to go kill themselves properly. You
> can see how they think its attention seeking and that people are
> cutting themselves for some sick kind of shock value. All in all
> though, it's like everything on the internet, there's some great
> stuff and some real crap and you have to sift through the crap to
> get the good stuff. If you can do that its fantastic and I must say I
> love using it. [Sam]

I have mentioned some of the main ways in which people who self-
injure use the internet. There are many more. These and others are
listed in the bibliography.

The impact of social change on self-injury

Oh my God! There's a whole world of people out there who are like me

How self-injury is viewed in society today is very different from its standing (largely based on research on clinical populations and narrow psychiatric conceptualisations) two decades ago. Celebrity ownership of the behaviour, public interest, infiltration of popular culture and the rise of the internet have all influenced how self-injury is understood in society. Some of the people who took part in this book did not know that others also self-injured. Anne was among those who reported having 'surfed' the internet in search of others like herself and like Tina, who became aware of others' self-injury from watching a television programme, was shocked to discover that she was not alone:

> I used the internet when I was about twelve or thirteen and I just realised 'Oh my God! There's a whole world of people out there who are like me'. [Anne]

The effect of finding out about other people who self-injure is often positive especially for those self-injuring for years in isolation. The impact on Sam is clear:

> I must say I have found it really helpful. I feel that I can confide in other people like me in total confidence and there is no possible chance that anyone can know who I am which makes it easier to say what you feel and be totally honest. Finding out about the websites has made me feel less lonely and less like a freak. I feel more confident in myself that this is the way I cope with bad stuff and I am sometimes even proud that I have come through it in my own way. I'm here to tell the tale and to be honest self-injury is part of the reason I've got this far. [Sam]

The accessibility to online relationships with others who self-injure has become a great tool in the battle against stigma. The 'space' desired by Sally to explore self-injury and related issues, anonymously, and in the virtual company of non-threatening, non-judgmental and likeminded individuals, has become available at the click of a computer mouse. Vast amounts of information can be accessed in a matter of seconds. Taking part in online discussions enables the user to exert an enormous amount of control which, especially for people who self-injure, can be an extremely welcome advantage. There is no pressure to take part in the discussion and they may end it at any time. Support can be accessed in a short space of time without having to travel. And according to Tantam and Huband (2009), the anonymity of online conversations encourages honesty and openness. They also point to additional therapeutic benefits of anxiety reduction in writing experiences down. Tina enjoys this aspect of using the internet:

> It's good in the sense that you don't have to be accountable to people cus you're never gona meet them. If you don't want to talk any more you just switch it off. Also you can say anything and not be embarrassed because they're never gona know who you are. And also, before when you thought you were alone in self-injury, it was lonely and you felt such a freak. Just the simple fact of knowing there are literally millions of people doing it makes it not feel that bad. I'm much more confident just knowing that I'm not as abnormal as I thought I was. [Tina]

Adler and Adler (2007) point out immensely positive benefits of structural shifting for those who self-injure:

> These changing social definitions have potentially profound implications for the lives of self-injurers. Mitigation of their social stigma has diminished self-injurers' rejection, isolation, and alienation... The changing social meanings of self-injury are carving out a place in society where participants may assert their understanding that self-injury is the product of their active choice and free will; that if not normalised, it is at least becoming more widely known and less stigmatised. (Adler and Adler, 2007:561)

In addition to acknowledging the potential benefits of finding other people who self-injure, some psychologists also caution that 'active participation in online communities may effectively substitute for the real work required to develop positive coping and healthy relationships' (Whitlock et al., 2007:2). And as Sam alluded to earlier, the freedom of speech afforded on the internet, as well as encouraging honesty and openness in a positive way, can also result in hurtful responses from others.

Self-injury, as we recognise it today, has travelled a long journey since its description in previous historical, biblical and medical sources. People who have been known to self-injure have been pilloried, shamed and feared. They have been assumed suicidal, accused of being manipulative, silenced and invalidated. Since the last decade of the twentieth century a hidden population of people who self-injure has emerged from obscurity. Ordinary people in the general population, whether they are known to medical authorities or not, are self-injuring. Often they are doing it in reaction to suffering, as a way to relieve psychological distress and it may become ritualised. The relationship between public and private faces of self-injury stigma is two-way. On a public level, structural changes that have brought the idea of self-injury to a world-wide audience have filtered down to the self-injuring individual and reduced his or her isolation and stigma. On a personal level, people who self-injure are refusing the stigma and promoting its greater acceptance in society. Regardless of the various viewpoints of self-injury, however, there is one certainty – Events of the past two decades have blasted the phenomenon well and truly into the forefront of society's attention, where it is guaranteed to remain.

Appendix

Pen-pictures of the people who took part

Pseudonym	Age at first self-injury	Age at interview	Brief synopsis of participants' information, including marital and employment status, forms and some functions of self-injury, main life traumas and other self-harming behaviours
John	18yrs	39yrs	Married with a five-year-old child. Employed as a researcher in a university. Grew up in highly controlled religious home environment. Self-injury began during break up of relationship with girlfriend who was also highly controlling. Discovered he is the son of his incestuous grandfather. Self-injury involves mostly cutting with a knife. 'Brings you back from point of suicide ... You feel better immediately'. Also tended to self-isolate and self-neglect. Has never been in contact with medical authorities in relation to self-injury. Not self-injuring at time of interview.
Jane	11yrs	23yrs	Single and unemployed. Grew up in highly controlled and invalidating home environment. 'I was a very sensitive child'. Bullied at school. Self-injures by cutting with blades and knives. 'When I cut I can think straight and carry on'. 'It feels natural to me ... as natural as eating my breakfast feels natural'. Diagnosed with

Continued

Pseudonym	Age at first self-injury	Age at interview	Brief synopsis of participants' information, including marital and employment status, forms and some functions of self-injury, main life traumas and other self-harming behaviours
			'borderline personality disorder'. Has abused alcohol and drugs. Poetry helps express herself positively. Not self-injuring at time of interview.
Anne	14yrs	19yrs	Attached, university student. Sexually abused by family friend. Bullied in secondary school. Suffered homophobia from peers in relation to her bisexuality. Growing up, she felt 'rejection, isolation and loneliness'. Self-injures by cutting with blades or burning with an iron. Self-injury releases anger and helps her to feel in control: 'This was my thing, you know? I was the one who could cause myself this pain, not other people'. Not self-injuring at time of interview.
Kathy	16yrs	30yrs	Single mother with five-year-old son. Adopted as a baby. 'Good' home environment with foster family, until, aged 12, she met 'scary looking' biological parents, who both had long-term mental health problems and were addicted to drugs and alcohol. Biological mother was physically and emotionally abusive. She forced Kathy to smoke cigarettes at age 14. Bullied at school. Self-injures by picking at skin and cutting. 'I can cope with the thoughts that are in my head when I do it'. Has been hospitalised after overdosing on painkillers. Diagnosed with a personality disorder. Also abuses

Continued

Pseudonym	Age at first self-injury	Age at interview	Brief synopsis of participants' information, including marital and employment status, forms and some functions of self-injury, main life traumas and other self-harming behaviours
			alcohol and drugs. Father of her son and his family trying to obtain custody of her child as they believe Kathy to be an 'unfit mother'. Still self-injuring at time of interview.
Nikea	13yrs	27yrs	Married with two children. Does not work outside home. Reported learning difficulties in school. Remembers having to take part in research and feeling like 'a guinea pig'. Relationship with mother was 'as good as it can be'. Bullied in secondary school. Felt 'lonely' growing up. Became a single teenage mother. Self-injured by cutting feet and other parts of body. Also has bulimic periods. Not injuring at time of interview.
Susan	40yrs	44yrs	Married with four grown up sons. Not employed outside home. Was an only child. Was 'adored' by parents. Alcoholic father. Death of parents resulted in first episode of self-injury. 'Couldn't cope with them dying'. Self-injury alternates between cutting and burning as a way to 'drain out all the emotional pain'. She also refers to self-injury as 'the lesser of two evils': 'I can go mad or do this. Nobody else need know'. Suffers from agrophobia and also abuses alcohol. Injuring at time of interview.
Tracey	14yrs	39yrs	Single, unemployed. Long-term sexual and physical abuse by father and invalidation from both parents

Continued

Pseudonym	Age at first self-injury	Age at interview	Brief synopsis of participants' information, including marital and employment status, forms and some functions of self-injury, main life traumas and other self-harming behaviours
			who did not tolerate expression of emotion from Tracey and eleven siblings. Realised she was being abused aged 11 after watching 'sex education video' in school. Took numerous overdoses of painkillers. Denied 'anything was wrong' to social workers because of fear of consequences. Abuse of alcohol and drugs from age of 11. Self-injures by cutting, which she reports is 'easier than crying and talking'. Cut words 'I am dead' into abdomen during one of many periods of hospitalisation. Relationship with family members is fragmented. Injuring at time of interview.
Nora	26yrs	30yrs	Single, laboratory technician. Raped aged 26. Witnessed death of 'best friend' at age three years, for which she feels self-blame. Self-injures by cutting with blades. Describes feelings at sight of blood when she self-injures: '…Aahh!…Everything is going to be OK'. Suffers from depression. Currently self-injuring.
Eve	31yrs	38yrs	Divorced, ex-teacher, with two children. Reported childhood as 'very, very happy'. Also referred to an 'authoritarian' father. Mental health problems after birth of second child. Is 'long term chronically mentally ill'. Has overdosed on tranquilisers and has been hospitalised as a result. Diagnosed as 'bipolar'. Poor mental health contributed to

Continued

Pseudonym	Age at first self-injury	Age at interview	Brief synopsis of participants' information, including marital and employment status, forms and some functions of self-injury, main life traumas and other self-harming behaviours
			marriage breakup. Self-injures with blades as 'a release of anxiety...the lesser of two evils [the other being suicide]'. Exercises excessively and has periods of starvation. Addicted to tranquilisers. Currently self-injuring.
Marie	14yrs	27yrs	Married, unemployed. Sexual abuse by (1) Cousin, (2) Teacher, (3) Neighbour. Controlled religious and invalidating childhood. Self-injures by cutting and burning. Describes release of 'anger and hate and frustration...blood flows, stuff flows with it'. Has been hospitalised. Diagnosed with borderline personality disorder. Abuse of alcohol and prescription and illicit drugs. Currently self-injuring.
Dawn	15yrs	21yrs	Student, in relationship. Had a 'strained' relationship with parents.'rejected' by extended family. Self-injures by cutting with blades and burning with an iron or hair straighteners. Expression of anger. Treated by psychiatrist for depression. Bullied at school. Felt 'ungainly' compared to 'smaller more petite girls at school'. Death of best friend by suicide when aged 15yrs. Low self-esteem. Abuse of alcohol. Currently occasionally self-injuring.
Tom	11yrs	23yrs	Single, office clerk. Bullied in school because of being overweight. Uncle murdered

Continued

Pseudonym	Age at first self-injury	Age at interview	Brief synopsis of participants' information, including marital and employment status, forms and some functions of self-injury, main life traumas and other self-harming behaviours
			grandfather and aunt when he was aged 10yrs. Self-injures by cutting with knives and blades, punching walls to relieve frustration and anger: 'I wanted pain. When I felt pain, it calmed me down'. History of psychiatric treatment for manic depression. Takes risks on motorbike and in car. Has been severely beaten up by loyalist paramilitaries. Abuse of illicit drugs. Self-injuring at time of interview.
Rachel	18yrs	26yrs	Married, office clerk expecting first baby. Rejected by father in childhood. Parents never married. Boyfriend died in car accident when they were both aged 15 years. Self-injured with blades and knives. 'I think it was a coping mechanism. It's something else to focus on. It was like…a release'. Alternates between self-injuring and bulimic periods. Has been treated with anti-depressants. Not self-injuring at time of interview.
Lena	14yrs	28yrs	Single, unemployed, hearing impaired. Sexual abuse by (1) institutional residents 2) brother-in-law. Highly controlled religious and invalidating home environment. Has vivid memories of mother being permanently institutionalised under mental health legislation when she was aged four. Alcoholic father. Lived in residential children's care and foster care. Lived with physically

Continued

Pseudonym	Age at first self-injury	Age at interview	Brief synopsis of participants' information, including marital and employment status, forms and some functions of self-injury, main life traumas and other self-harming behaviours
			(and emotionally abusive sister and sexually, physically and emotionally abusive brother-in-law. Self-injured with knives to 'ease emotional pain'. Received medical and psychiatric treatment relating to self-injury. Other forms of self-harm – anorexic periods and self neglect. Currently self-injuring.
Steve	14yrs	40yrs	Divorced, unemployed ex-soldier. Sexual abuse by institutional carer. Physical and emotional abuse and invalidation by stepmother and houseparents. Self-injures by cutting with razor blades. 'It feels brilliant, absolute pure relief and calm'. Wife left marriage and began relationship with his 'best friend'. Poor relationship with siblings. Felt 'rejection, rejection, rejection … my whole life … That's the one way I would describe why I self-harm … rejection'. Has received medical and psychiatric treatment relating to self-injury. Also tends to have periods of self-neglect, going without food in particular. Self-injuring regularly at time of interview.
Lisa	11yrs	28yrs	Single, unemployed. Sexual abuse by (1) uncle, (2) cousin and (3) boyfriend. 'Couldn't talk to parents'. Felt neglected by them. Self-injury by blades to 'get rid of bad feeling'. Family unrest due to reporting of abuse perpetrated by uncle and cousin. Abuse of alcohol

Continued

Pseudonym	Age at first self-injury	Age at interview	Brief synopsis of participants' information, including marital and employment status, forms and some functions of self-injury, main life traumas and other self-harming behaviours
			and drugs. Has been hospitalised due to anorexia. Has phobia of mirrors. Currently self-injuring.
Laura	15yrs	19yrs	Single, unemployed. Sexual abuse by uncle at age of 11 years. Cuts herself with blades: 'It's not suicidal or attention seeking. It's my way of dealing with the abuse'. Was hospitalised when family found out about self-injury. Family still unaware of sexual abuse by uncle. Self-injuring regularly at time of interview.
Ella	31yrs	39yrs	Divorced with three grown-up sons. Repeated sexual abuse by father from age three years until his death when she was sixteen. Controlled religious and invalidating home environment. Revealed father's abuse to mother but it continued. Suffers from dissociative periods, flashbacks, social paralysis. Self-injures with blades to 'feel such a relief…calm and in control'. Also abuses drugs and alcohol. Had not self-injured for a number of months prior to interview.
Sally	11yrs	34yrs	Single, disabled, unemployed. Repeated sexual abuse by brother from childhood to early teens. Invalidating home environment. Self-injures by cutting with blades. 'It was damage limitation. It stopped me from killing myself. If I didn't do it I would not be here…I would be dead.' Disclosure

Continued

Pseudonym	Age at first self-injury	Age at interview	Brief synopsis of participants' information, including marital and employment status, forms and some functions of self-injury, main life traumas and other self-harming behaviours
			of sexual abuse divided family. Has been hospitalised. Suffers from depression. Writes poetry, takes part in research, has spoken at a conference on 'self-harm' and has been interviewed by media in relation to self-injury and court case regarding her abusive brother. Self-injuring at time of interview.
Mike	14yrs	40yrs	Single, clergyman. Sexual abuse by three separate family friends. Self-injured by cutting with knives and punching himself. 'For me it was a way of expressing...trying to put out...an outward form of the interior agony that was going on'. It also helped 'end periods of total disembodiment...To inflict pain on yourself is like a way to bring you back into the world.'. Received psychological counselling. Also had periods of bulimia. Not currently self-injuring.
Sam	12yrs	42yrs	Married sales manager with four children. Sexual abuse by uncle. Physical and emotional abuse and neglect by mother. Invalidating childhood home environment. Self-injured by cutting with blades and biting tongue. 'It helps me stay in control, when the bad thoughts start. If I didn't have self-injury...I don't know what way I would have ended up'. Being treated with antidepressants for chronic depression and anxiety. Contact with family of origin is

Continued

Pseudonym	Age at first self-injury	Age at interview	Brief synopsis of participants' information, including marital and employment status, forms and some functions of self-injury, main life traumas and other self-harming behaviours
			limited and relationships therein are 'strained'. Has a tendency to binge drink. Not currently self-injuring.
Tina	15yrs	39yrs	Married preschool assistant with four children. Physical and emotional neglect by parents. Isolated and bullied at school. Invalidating home environment. Self-injures by cutting with blades. 'When I cut myself, I feel like the pressure and anxiety is released and then I can get up and make the dinner and function as a wife and mother'. Has been bulimic since mid-teens. Self-injuring occasionally at time of interview.
Aoife	13yrs	28yrs	Divorced, in relationship, community volunteer, with three children under age ten. Childhood was marked by invalidation and physical neglect at home and sexual abuse by a neighbour. Was married to an abusive husband for eight years. Aoife instigated separation and divorce. In new relationship with divorced man. Self-injury involves cutting with blades: 'For me, self-injury is a way to stay alive. OK, its not exactly a healthy way to cope, but for some people it's the only way they have'. Also is bulimic and abuses alcohol and painkillers. Not currently self-injuring.
Molly	12yrs	32yrs	Single, office clerk. Father physically and emotionally abusive. 'My father never loved me. He told me that to my face. He favoured my sister'.

Continued

Pseudonym	Age at first self-injury	Age at interview	Brief synopsis of participants' information, including marital and employment status, forms and some functions of self-injury, main life traumas and other self-harming behaviours
			Father long-term institutionalisation as chronic 'manic depressant'. Has made 'sexual advances' towards her in adulthood. Parents divorced in Molly's childhood. Sexual abuse by neighbour. 'Self-harm is my best friend. It helps me get through'. Sexually promiscuous and has had a number of sexual relationships with married men. Has had three abortions. Alternates between anorexic, bulimic and self-injuring periods. Diagnosed as 'multi impulsive bulimic associated with alcohol, sex and self-injury'. Currently self-injuring.
Deirdre	12yrs	38yrs	Married, social worker, with two children. Born as the result of her mother being raped by a stranger. Was given up for adoption and placed with adoptive family. Sexual abuse by adoptive brother. Physical and emotional abuse and neglect by adoptive mother. Invalidating home environment. Self-injures by cutting and burning with blades, matches and cigarettes lighters. 'It's such a great feeling... It's like releasing a pressure valve, of anger, fear and frustration'. Binge drinks, occasionally takes illicit drugs, sexually promiscuous. Occasionally self-injuring at time of interview.

Data:
Interviews = 25 (one with each participant)
Participants = males x 25, females x 20
Diaries x 3 (Susan, Tina, Sam)
Collections of poetry x 3 (Jane, Dawn, Sally)

Bibliography

A man called horse (1970) [Film clip] Available at: http://www.youtube.com/watch?v=z829cL9spho. Accessed on 10 March 2010.

Abrams, L. S. and Gordon, A. L.(2003) Self-harm narratives of urban and suburban women. *Affilia* 18(4): 429–44.

Adler, P. A. and Adler, P. (2005) Self-injurers as loners: The social organisation of solitary deviance. *Deviant behaviour* 26: 345–78.

Adler, P. A. and Adler, P. (2007) The demedicalisation of self-injury: From psychopathology to sociological deviance. *Journal of contemporary ethnography* 36(5): 537–70.

Adler, P. A. and Adler, P. (2011) *The tender cut: Inside the hidden world of self-injury.* New York: New York University Press.

Alderman, T. (1997) *The scarred soul: Understanding and ending self-inflicted violence.* Oakland: New Harbinger.

Almack, K. (2007) Out and about: Negotiating the layers of being out in the process of disclosure of lesbian parenthood. *Sociological research online,* 12(1), Available at http://www.socresonline.org.uk/12/1/almack.html. Accessed on 10 March 2010.

American Psychiatric Association (2000) *Diagnostic and statistical manual of mental disorders,* 4th ed. Text revised. Washington DC: American Psychiatric Association.

Andover, M. S., Pepper, C. M., Ryabchenko, K. A., Orrico, E. G. and Gibb, B. E. (2005) Self-mutilation and symptoms of depression, anxiety and borderline personality disorder. *Suicide and life-threatening behaviour* 35: 581–91.

Arnold, L. (1995) *Women and self-injury: A survey of 76 women.* Bristol: Bristol Crisis Service for Women.

Arnold, L. and Magill, A. (2000) *Making sense of self-harm.* London: The Basement Project Publications.

Atchison, M. and McFarlane, A. C. (1994) A review of dissociation and dissociative disorders. *Aust/ NZ J psychiatry* 28: 591–9.

Babiker, G. and Arnold, L. (1997) *The language of injury: Comprehending self-mutilation.* Leicester: British psychological society.

BBC Panorama interview with Princess Diana (1995). Online video. Available at: http://www.youtube.com/watch?v=Zlxs_JG1dDA&feature=related Accessed on 6 April 2011.

Bhugra, D., Singh, J., Fellow-Smith, E. and Bayliss, C. (2002). Deliberate self-harm in adolescents. A case study among two ethnic groups. *European journal of psychiatry* 16(3): 145–51.

Bissland, J. H. and Munger, R. (1985) Implications of changing attitudes toward mental illness. *Journal of social psychology* 125: 515–17.

Bowen, A. C. L. and John, A. M. H. (2001) Gender differences in presentation and conceptualisation of adolescent self-injurious behaviour: Implications for therapeutic practice. *Counselling psychology quarterly* 14: 357–79.

Briere, J. and Gill, E. (1998) Self-mutilation in clinical and general population samples: Prevalence, correlates and functions. *American journal of orthopsychiatry* 68: 609–20.

Bristol Crisis Service for Women (2000) *Understanding self-injury.* Bristol: Bristol Crisis Service for Women.

Brodsky, B. S., Cliotre, M. and Dulit, R. A. (1995) The relationship of dissociation to self-mutilation and childhood abuse in borderline personality disorder. *American journal of psychiatry* 152: 1788–92.

Brown, L. S. and Bryan, T. C. (2007) Feminist therapy with people who self-inflict violence. *Journal of clinical psychology: In session* 63(11): 1121–33.

Burstow, B. (1992) *Radical feminist therapy.* London: Sage.

Carlson, N. (2011). *Goldman to clients: Facebook has 600 million users.* Business Insider

Available at: http://www.msnbc.msn.com/id/40929239/ns/technology_and_science-tech_and_gadgets/. Accessed on 8 April 2011.

Carter, W. E. (1977) The Aymara and the role of alcohol in human society. In: B. M. Du Toit (ed.) *Drugs, rituals and altered states of consciousness,* pp. 101–10. Rotterdam: Balkema.

Chu, J., Frey, L., Ganzel, B. and Matthews, J. (1999) Memories of childhood abuse: Dissociation, amnesia and corroboration. *American journal of psychiatry* 156(5): 749–55. Retrieved on 16 Jan 2008.

Claes, L., Vandereycken, W. and Vertommen, H. (2007) Self-injury in female versus male psychiatric patients: A comparison of characteristics, psychopathology and aggression regulation. *Personality and individual differences* 42(4): 611–21.

Connors, R. E. (2000) Self-injury: Psychotherapy with people who engage in self-inflicted violence. New Jersey: Aronson Inc.

Cooley, C. H. (1964) *Human nature and the social order.* New York: Schocken.

Cooper, J., Kapur, N., Webb, R., Lawlor, M., Guthrie, E., Mackway-Jones, K. and Appleby, L. (2005) Suicide after deliberate self-harm: A four year cohort study. *American journal of psychiatry* 162: 297–303.

Crowe, M. and Bunclarke, J. (2000) Repeated self-injury and its management. *International review of psychiatry* 12(1): 48–53.

Dallam, S. J. (1997) The identification and management of self-mutilating patients in primary care. *The nurse practitioner* 22: 151–64.

Darche, M. A. (1990) Psychological factors differentiating self-mutilating and non-self-mutilating adolescent inpatient females. *The psychiatric hospital* 21: 31–5.

Deiter, P. J., Nicholls, S. S. and Pearlman, L. A. (2000) Self-injury and self capacities: Assisting an individual in crisis. *Journal of clinical psychology* 56(9): 1173–91.

Digital spy (2011) Soap scoop: E'dale self-harm, Tamwar romance, Corrie temptress. Available at: http://www.digitalspy.co.uk/soaps/scoop/a286449/

edale-self-harm-tamwar-romance-corrie-temptress.html. Accessed on 11 April 2011.

Durkheim, E. (1971) *The elementary forms of religious life.* London: George Allen and Unwin Ltd.

Favazza, A. R. (1989) Why patients mutilate themselves. *Hospital and community psychiatry* 40: 137–45.

Favazza, A. R. (1996) *Bodies under siege: Self-mutilation and body modification in culture and* psychiatry, 2nd ed. Baltimore: The John Hopkins University Press.

Favazza, A. R. (1998) The coming of age of self-mutilation. *The journal of nervous and mental disease* 186(5): 259–68.

Favazza, A. R. and Conterio, K. (1988) The plight of chronic self-mutilators. *Community mental health journal* 24.

Favazza, A. R. and Rosenthal, R. J. (1993) Diagnostic issues in self-mutilation. *Hospital and community psychiatry* 44: 134–41.

Favazza, A. R. and Conterio, K. (1989) Habitual female self-mutilators. *Acta psychiatry Scand.* 79: 283–9.

Favazza, A. R., DeRosear, L. and Conterio, K. (1989) Self-mutilation and eating disorders. *Suicide and life-threatening behaviour* 19: 352–61.

Feldman, M. D. (1988) The challenge of self-mutilation: A review. *Comprehensive psychiatry* 29(3): 252–69.

Firstsigns (2010) *Self-injury guidance and network support.* Available at: http://www.firstsigns.org.uk/. Accessed on 1 March 2010.

Gabrielle (2011) *Famous self-injurers.* Available at: http://www.self-injury.net. Accessed on 7 April 2011.

Garrison, C. Z., Addy, C. L., McKeown, R. E. and Cuffe, S. P. (1993) Nonsuicidal physically self-damaging acts in adolescents. *Journal of child & family studies* 2: 339–52.

Girl interrupted [DVD] (2000) USA: Columbia Tristar.

Glaser, B. and Strauss, A. (1968) *Time for dying.* Chicago: Adline.

Glaser, B. and Strauss, A. (1971) *Status passage.* Chicago: Aldine Publishing Co.

Goffman, E. (1963) *Stigma: Notes on the management of spoiled identity.* New York: Simon and Schuster Inc.

Goffman, E. (1967) *Interaction ritual: Essays on face to face behaviour.* New York: Pantheon books.

Good to know magazine. Available at: http://www.goodtoknow.co.uk/family/256247/Self-harm-in-kids--Is-it-just-attention-seeking-. Accessed on 7 April 2011.

Gratz, K. L. (2001) Measurement of deliberate self-harm: Preliminary data on the deliberate self-harm inventory. *Journal of psychopathology and behavioural assessment* 23: 253–63.

Gratz, K. L. (2006) Risk factors for deliberate self-harm among female college students: The role and interaction of childhood maltreatment, emotional inexpressivity, and affect intensity/reactivity. *American journal of orthopsychiatry* 76(2): 238–50.

Gratz, K. L. (2007) Targeting emotion dysregulation in the treatment of self-injury. *Journal of clinical psychology: In session* 63(11): 1091–103.

Gratz, K. L., Conrad, S. D. and Roemer, L. (2002) Risk factors for deliberate self-harm among college students. *American journal of orthopsychiatry* 72: 128–40.

Gratz, K. L. and Roemer, L. (2004) Multidimensional assessment of emotion regulation and dysregulation: Development, factor structure, and initial validation of the difficulties in emotion regulation scale. *Journal of psychopathology and behavioural assessment* 26: 41–54.

Green, A. H. (1978) Self-destructive behaviour in battered children. *American journal of psychiatry* 135: 579–82.

Green, G. and Sobo, E. (2000) *The endangered self: Managing the social risks of HIV.* London: Routledge.

Grossman, R. and Siever, L. (2001) Impulsive self-injurious behaviours, neurobiology and psychopharmacology. In D. Simeon and E. Hollander (eds) *Self-injurious behaviours: Assessment and treatment.* Washingtom DC: American psychiatric Association.

Grund, J. P. (1993) *Drug use as social ritual: Functionality, symbolism and determinants of self-regulation.* Rotterdam: Instituut voor Verslavingsonderzoek. The concept of ritualisation.

Haines, J. and Williams, C. L. (1997) Coping and problem solving of self-mutilators. *Journal of clinical psychology* 53(2): 177–86.

Harris, J. (2000) Self-harm: Cutting the bad out of me. *Qualitative health research* 10(2): 164–73.

Harter, S. (1999) Symbolic interactionism revised: Potential liabilities for the self constructed in the crucible of interpersonal relationships. *Merrill-Palmer quarterly.*

Hawton, K. (2000) Sex and suicide: Gender differences in suicidal behaviour. *British journal of psychiatry* 177: 484–5.

Hawton, K. and Catalan, J. (1987) *Attempted suicide: A practical guide to its nature and management,* 2nd ed. Oxford: Oxford University Press.

Hawton, K. and James, A. (2005) Suicide and deliberate self harm in young people. *British medical journal* 330: 891–4.

Hawton, K., Arensman, E., Townsend, E., Bremner, S., Feldman, E., Goldney, R., Gunnell, D., Hazell, P., Van Heeringen, K., House, A., Owens, D., Sakinofsky, I. and Traskman-Bendz, L. (1998) Deliberate self-harm: Systematic review of efficacy of psychosocial and pharmacological treatments in preventing repetition. *British medical journal* 317(7156): 441.

Hawton, K., Fagg, J., Simkin, S., Bale, E. and Bond, A. (2000) Deliberate self-harm in Oxford, 1985–1995. *Journal of adolescence* 23(1): 47–55.

Hawton, K., Rodham, K., Evans, E. and Weatherall, R. (2002) Deliberate self harm in adolescents: Self-report survey in schools in England. *British medical journal* 325: 1207– 11.

Hawton, K., Rodham, K. and Evans, E. (2006) *By their own young hand: Deliberate self-harm and suicide ideas in adolescence.* London: Jessica Kingsley.

Herman, J. (1986) *Crazies in the community: An ethnographic study of ex-psychiatric clients in Canadian society.* PhD thesis. McMaster University. Hamilton Ontario, Canada.

Herman, J. (1992) *Trauma and recovery.* London: Harper Collins.

Herman, J. (1993) Return to sender: Reintegrative stigma-management strat-egies of ex-psychiatric patients. *Journal of contemporary ethnography* 22(3): 295–330.

Herpertz, S. (1995) Self-injurious behaviour: Psychopathological and nosolo-gical characteristics in subtypes of self-injurers. *Acta Psychiatric Scandanavia* 91: 57–68.

Herpertz, S., Sass, H. and Favazza, A. R. (1997) Impulsivity in self-mutila-tive behaviour: Psychometric and biological findings. *Journal of psychiatric research* 31: 451–65.

Hodgson, S. (2004) Cutting through the silence: A sociological construction of self-injury. *Sociological inquiry* 74(2): 162–79.

Holmes, K. (2007) *Black, white and gold: My autobiography.* London: Virgin books Ltd.

Hurry, J. (2000) Deliberate self-harm in children and adolescents. *International review of psychiatry* 12(1): 31–6.

Hyman, J. W. (1999) *Women living with self-injury.* Philadelphia: Temple University press.

Isacsson, G. and Rich, C. L. (2001) Management of patients who deliberately harm themselves. *British medical journal* 322: 213–15.

Jackson, S. W. (2008) A history of melancholia and depression. In: E. R. Wallace and J. Gach (eds) *A history of psychiatry and medical psychology,* pp. 443–60. New York: Springer.

Jacoby, A. (1994) Felt versus enacted stigma: A concept revisited. *Social science and medicine* 38(2): 269–74.

Jayloe, B. (2003) Exploring the perspectives of men who self-harm. *Learning in health and social care* 2(2): 83–91.

Jeffreys, S. (2000). 'Body art' and social status: Cutting tattooing and pierc-ing from a feminist perspective. *Feminism and psychology* 10: 409–29.

Johnson, R. and Chernoff, N. (2002) Opening a vein: Inmate poetry and the prison experience. *The prison journal* 82(2): 141–67.

Johnstone, L. (1997) Self-injury and the psychiatric response. *Feminism and psychology* 7(3): 421–6.

Johnstone, N. (2010) *Johnny Depp: The illustrated biography.* London: Carlton Books.

Kenyon, G. M. (1996) Ethical issues in aging and biography. *Aging and society* 16: 659–75.

Kettlewell, C. (2000) *Skin game.* New York: St Martin's Griffin.

Klonsky, D. E. (2007) The functions of deliberate self-injury: A review of the evidence. *Clinical psychology review* 27: 226–39.

Klonsky, D. E. and Muehlenkamp, J. L. (2007) Self-injury: A research review for the practitioner. *Journal of clinical psychology: In session* 63(11): 1045–56.

Klonsky, D. E., Oltmanns, T. F. and Turkheimer, E. (2003) Deliberate self-harm in a non-clinical population: Prevalence and psychological corre-lates. *American journal of psychiatry* 160: 1501–8.

Kokaliari, E. (2004). *Deliberate Self-Injury: An Investigation of the Prevalence and Psychosocial Meanings in a Non-Clinical Female College Population.* Dissertation. Smith College.

Langbehn, D. R. and Pfohl, B. (1993) Clinical correlates of self-mutilation among psychiatric inpatients. *Annals of clinical psychiatry* 5: 45–51.

Laye-Gindhu, A. and Schonert-Reichl, K. A. (2005) Non-suicidal self-harm among community adolescents: Understanding the 'whats' and 'whys' of self-harm. *Journal of youth and adolescence* 34: 447–57.

Leibenluft, E., Gardner, D. L. and Cowdry, R. W. (1987) The inner experience of the borderline self-injurer. *Journal of personality disorders* 1(4): 317–24.

Lenhart, A., Madden, M. and Hitlin, P. (2005) Teens and technology. Pew internet and American life project. Available at http://www.pewinternet.org/Reports/2005/Teens-and-Technology.aspx. Accessed on 1 March 2010.

Levenkron, S. (1998) *The luckiest girl in the world: A young skater battles her self-destructive impulses.* New York: Penguin.

Liebling, H., Chipcase, H. and Velangi, R. (1997) Why do women harm themselves? – surviving special hospitals. *Feminism and psychology* 7(3): 427–37.

Linehan, M. M. (1993) *Cognitive-behavioural treatment of borderline personality disorder.* New York: The Guilford Press.

Lundh, L. G., Karim, J. and Quilisch, E. (2007) Deliberate self-harm in 15 year old adolescents: A pilot study with a modified version of the deliberate self-harm inventory. *Scandinavian journal of psychology* 48: 33–41.

McBride, A. J., Pates, R. M., Arnold, K. and Ball, N. (2001) Needle fixation, the drug user's perspective: A qualitative study. *Addiction* 96(7): 1049–58.

McElrath, K. (2006) Booting and flushing: Needle rituals and risk for blood-borne viruses. *Journal of substance use* 11: 177–89.

McLane, J. (1996) The voice on the skin: Self-mutilation and Merleau-Ponty's theory of language. *Hypathia* 11(4): 107–19.

Manic Street Preachers (2011) Official website. Available at: http://www.manicstreetpreachers.com/global/discography/all/albums/all/journal_for_plague_lovers_1. Accessed on 7 April 2011.

Marshall, H. and Yazdani, A. (1999) Locating culture in accounting for self-harm amongst Asian young women. *Journal of community and applied social psychology* 9(6): 413–33.

Martinson, D. (1998) *Etiology of self-injury.* Available at http://www.palace.net/~llama/selfinjury. Accessed on 7 March 2010.

Mead, G. H. (1934) *Mind, self and society.* Chicago: Chicago University Press.

Melzer, H., Jenkins, R., Singleton, N., Charton, J. and Yar, M. (1999) Non fatal suicidal behaviour among prisoners. London: ONS.

Mercer, R. (2007) *Angelina Jolie: The biography.* London: John Blake Publishing Ltd.

Merton, R. K. (1995) The Thomas Theorem and the Matthew Effect. *Social Forces* 74(2): 379–424.

Miall, C. E. (1989) Authenticity and the disclosure of the information preserve: The case of adoptive parenthood. *Qualitative sociology* 12: 279–302.

Miller, D. (1994) *Women who hurt themselves: A book of hope and understanding.* New York: Basic books.

Mills, C. Wright (1940) 'situated Actions and Vocabularies of Motive'. *American Sociological Review* 5: 904–13.

Miniwatts Marketing Group (2010). Available at http://www.internetworld-stats.com/top2000.htm. Accessed on 5 April 2011.

Muehlenkamp, J. J. and Gutierrez, P. M. (2004). An investigation of differences between self-injurious behavior and suicide attempts in a sample of adolescents. *Suicide & Life-Threatening Behavior* 34(12–24).

Nafisi, N. and Stanley, B. (2007) Developing and maintaining the therapeutic alliance with self-injuring patients. *Journal of clinical psychology: In session* 63(11): 1069–79.

National Institute for Clinical Excellence (NICE) (2004) *Self-harm: The short-term physical and psychological management and secondary prevention of self-harm in primary and secondary care.* Leicester: The British psychological society.

Nixon, M. K. and Heath, N. L. (2009). *Self-injury in youth: The essential guide to assessment and intervention.* New York, NY: Routledge Press.

Nock, M. K. and Prinstein, M. J. (2004) A functional approach to the assessment of self-mutilative behaviour. *Journal of consulting and clinical psychology* 72: 885–90.

Nock, M. K., Joiner, T. E., Gordon, K. H., Lloyd-Richardson, E. and Prinstein, M. J. (2006) Non-suicidal self-injury among adolescents: Diagnostic correlates and relation to suicide attempts. *Psychiatry research* 144: 65–72.

Nock, M. K., Teper, R. and Hollander, M. (2007) Psychological treatment of self-injury among adolescents. *Journal of clinical psychology: In session* 63(11): 1081–9.

Norris, M. L., Boydell, K. M., Pinhas, L. and Katman, D. K. (2006) Ana and the internet: A review of pro-anorexic websites. *International journal of eating disorders* 39: 443–7.

Office for National statistics (2009) *Internet Access.* Available at: http://www.statistics.gov.uk/cci/nugget.asp?ID=8. Accessed on 1 March 2010.

Ogundipe, L. O. (1999) Suicide attempts vs deliberate self-harm. *British journal of psychiatry* 175: 90.

Page, R. M. (1984) *Stigma: Concepts in social policy.* Boston: Routledge.

Park, K. (2002) Stigma management among the voluntary childless. *Sociological perspectives* 45(1): 21–45.

Partridge, W. L. (1977) Transformation and redundancy in ritual: A case from Columbia. In B. M. Du Toit (ed.) *Drugs, rituals and altered states of consciousness.* Rotterdam: Balkema.

Pates, R. (2001) A case of needle fixation. *Journal of substance use* 6: 202–6.

Pattison, E. M. and Kahan, J. (1983) The deliberate self-harm syndrome. *American journal of psychiatry* 140: 867–72.

Pembroke, L. R. (1994) *Self-harm: Perspectives from personal experience.* London: Survivors Speak Out.

Pfuhl, E. H. Jr (1986) *The deviance process,* 2nd ed. Belmont, CA: Wadsworth.

Pies, R. W. and Popli, A. P. (1995) Self-injurous behaviour: Pathophysiology and implications for treatment. *Journal of clinical psychiatry* 56: 580–8.

Portman, A. (1961) *Animals as social beings.* New York: Viking Press.

Prins, E. (1995) *Maturing out: An empirical study of personal histories and processes in hard-drug addiction.* Doctoral dissertation, Erasmus University Rotterdam.

Radcliffe-Brown, A. R. (1952) *Structure and function in primitive society.* London: Cohen and West Ltd.

Riemann, G. and Schütze, F. (2005) 'Trajectory' as a basic theoretical concept for suffering and disorderly social processes. In R. Miller (ed.) *Biographical Research Methods Vol III.* London: Sage Publications Ltd.

Riessman, C. K. (2000) Stigma and everyday resistance practices: Childless women in south India. *Gender and society* 14(1): 111–35.

Robinson, A. and Duffy, J. (1989) A comparison of self-injury and self-poisoning from the regional poisoning treatment centre. Edinburgh. *Acta Psychiatra Scandinavica* 80: 272–9.

Rosenthal, G. (2003) The healing effects of storytelling on the conditions of curative storytelling in the context of research and counselling. *Qualitative Enquiry* 9(6): 915–33.

Ross, S. and Heath, N. (2002) A study of the frequency of self-mutilation in a community sample of adolescents. *Journal of youth and adolescence* 31: 67–77.

Royal College of Psychiatrists (2009) Physical activity and mental health [Online]. Available at http://www.rcpsych.ac.uk/mentalhealthinfoforall/treatments/physicalactivity.aspx. Accessed on 21 March 2010.

Scambler, G. and Hopkins, A. (1986) Being epileptic: Coming to terms with stigma. *Sociology of health and illness* 8(1): 26–43.

Schaffer, C. B., Carroll, J. and Abramowitz, S. I. (1982) Self-mutilation and the borderline personality. *Journal of nervous mental disorders* 170: 468–73.

Schneider, J. W. and Conrad, P. (1980) In the closet with illness: Epilepsy, stigma potential and information control. *Social problems* 28: 32–44.

Schütze, F. (1981) Prozeßstrukturen des Lebensablaufs. In: Joachim Matthes, Arno Pfeifenberger and Manfred Stosberg (eds) *Biographie in handlungswissenschaftlicher Perspektive,* pp. 67–156. Nurnberg:Verlag der Nurnberg Forschungsvereinigung.

Schütze, F. (1982) Narrative representation kollektiver schicksalsbetroffenheit. In: E. Lammert (ed.) *Erzahlforschung, ein symposium.* Metzler, Stuttgart.

Scott, M. B. and Lyman, S. M. (1968) Accounts. *American sociological review* 33(1): 46–62.

Secretary (DVD) (2002) Motion picture. USA: Prism Leisure Corporation.

Sharkey, V. (2003) Self-wounding: A literature review. *Mental health practice* 6: 35–7.

Shearer, S. L. (1994) Phenomenology of self-injury among inpatient women with borderline personality disorder. *Journal of nervous mental disorders* 182: 524–6.

Sia (2011) Online lyrics. Available at: http://www.sing365.com/music/lyric.nsf/breathe-me-lyrics-sia/5baf785a295a848248256f2b00129392. Accessed on 7 April 2011.

Simeon, D., Stanley, B., Frances, A., Mann, J. J., Winchel, R. and Stanley, M. (1992) Self-mutilation in personality disorders: Psychological and biological correlates. *American journal of psychiatry* 149(2): 221–6.

Smith, G., Cox, D. and Saradjian, J. (1998) *Women and self-harm.* London: The Women's Press.

Soloff, P. H., Lis, J. A., Kelly, T., Cornelius, J. and Ulrich, R. (1994) Self-mutilation and suicidal behaviour in borderline personality disorder. *Journal of personality disorders* 8: 257–67.

Solomon, Y. and Farrand, J. (1996) 'Why don't you do it properly?' Young women who self-injure. *Journal of adolescence* 19(2): 111–19.

Spandler, H. (1996) *Who's hurting who? Young people, self-harm and suicide.* Manchester: 42nd Street.

Steinberg, M. (1994) Systematizing dissociation: Symptomatology and diagnostic assessment. In: D. Spiegel (ed.) *Dissociation: Culture, mind and body.*

Strauss, A. and Glaser, B. (1970) *Anguish: The case history of a dying trajectory.* Mill Valley, CA: The sociological press.

Strong, M. (1998) *A bright red scream: Self-mutilation and the language of pain.* New York: Penguin Putnam.

Sutherland, E. H. (1939) *Principles of criminology*, 3rd ed. Philadelphia: J.B. Lippincott

Sutton, J. (1999) *Healing the hurt within: Understand and relieve the suffering behind self-destructive behaviour.* Oxford: Pathways.

Suyemoto, K. L. and MacDonald, M. L. (1995) Self-cutting in female adolescents. *Psychotherapy* 32: 162–71.

Sykes, G. M. and Matza, D. (1957) Techniques of neutralization: A theory of delinquency. *American sociological review* 22: 664–70.

Tantam, D. and Huband, N. (2009) *Understanding repeated self-injury: A multidisciplinary approach.* Basingstoke: Palgrave Macmillan.

Tantam, D. and Whittaker, J. (1992) Personality disorder and self-wounding. *British Journal of Psychiatry* 161: 451–64.

The Social Network (DVD) (2011) USA: Sony Pictures Home Entertainment

Thomas, P. (1998) Foreword In: Dace et al. *The hurt yourself less workbook*, pp. 3–5. London: National Self-harm Network.

Trepal, H. C. (2010) Exploring self-injury through a relational cultural lens. *Journal of counselling and development.* Retrieved 3 February 2011 from http://www.faqs.org/periodicals/201010/2138475441.html

TV.Com (2001). *Hollyoaks let loose.* Hollyoaks episode 12 recap. Available at: http://www.tv.com/hollyoaks-let-loose/episode-twelve/episode/492692/recap.html. Accessed on 7 April 2011.

Van der Kolk, B. A. and Van der Hart, O. (1989) The dissociation theory of Pierre Janet. *Journal of traumatic stress* 2: 397–412.

Van der Kolk, B. A., Perry, J. C. and Herman, J. L. (1991) Childhood origins of self-destructive behaviour. *American journal of psychiatry* 148: 1665–71.

Wallace A. F. C. (1966) *Religion: An anthropological view.* New York: Random House.

Walsh, B. W. (2007) Clinical assessment of self-injury: A practical guide. *Journal of clinical psychology: In session* 63(11): 1057–68.

Walsh, B. W. (2008) *Treating self-injury: A practical guide.* New York: Guilford press.

Walsh, B. W. and Rosen, P. M. (1988) *Self-mutilation: Theory, research and treatment.* New York: Guilford press.

Whitlock, J. L. (2010) What is self-injury. [Fact sheet] *Cornell Research Program on Self-Injurious Behavior in Adolescents and Young Adults.* Available at http://crpsib.com/factsheet_aboutsi.asp. Accessed on 19 March 2010.

Whitlock, J. L., Lader, W. and Conterio, K. (2007) The internet and self-injury: What psychotherapists should know. Available at http://www.crpsib.com/userfiles/File/Pub1.pdf. Accessed on 4 February 2010.

Whitlock, J. L., Eckenrode, J. E. and Silverman, D. (2006a) The epidemiology of self-injurious behaviour in a college population. *Pediatrics* 117(6): 1939–48.

Whitlock, J. L., Powers, J. L. and Eckenrode, J. (2006b) The virtual cutting edge: The internet and adolescent self-injury. *Developmental psychology* 43(3): 1–11.

Wilkins, S. (1965) *Social deviance*. London: Tavistock.

World Health Organisation (1992) *The ICD-10 Classification of Mental and Behavioural Disorders: Clinical Descriptions and Diagnostic Guidelines*. Geneva: World Health Organisation.

World Health Organisation (2007) *The International Classification of Disease* (2007) (10th edition) (ICD-10). Available at http://www.who.int/classifications/icd/en/ (Home page). Accessed on 10 March 2010.

Youtube (2011) Available at http://www.youtube.com

Angelina Jolie interview http://www.youtube.com/watch?v=IW1Ay4u5JDE Accessed on 6 April 2011.

Good Morning Television (GMTV) (2007) Self-injury awareness day presented by Lorraine Kelly. Available at: http://www.youtube.com/watch?v=FBURspHpB9E&feature=related. Accessed on 7 April 2011.

Self harm: Part One. *The Wright Stuff*. Channel 5. http://www.youtube.com/watch?v=x6C31FWLWqQ&feature=fvwrel Accessed on 7 April 2011.

Self harm: Part Two. *The Wright Stuff*. Channel 5. http://www.youtube.com/watch?v=ToefbP2Grfc&feature=fvwrel Accessed on7 April 2011.

Zlotnick, C., Shea, M. T., Pearlstein, T., Simpson, E., Costello, E. and Begin, A. (1996) The relationship between dissociative symptoms, alexithymia, impulsivity, sexual abuse, and self-mutilation. *Comprehensive psychiatry* 37: 12–16.

Zoroglu, S. S., Tuzun, U., Sar, V., Tutkun, H., Savas, H. A., Ozturk, M. et al. (2003) Suicide attempts and self-mutilation among Turkish high school students in relation to abuse, neglect and dissociation. *Psychiatry and clinical neurosciences* 57: 119–26.

Some websites used by people who self-injure

www.bebo.com
www.facebook.com
www.fortysecondstreet.org.uk
www.firstsigns.org.uk
www.mind.org.uk
www.myspace.com
www.nshn.co.uk
www.palace.net
www.samaritans.com

Index